THE SOUND OF DREAMS REMEMBERED

Books by Al Young

Dancing (poems)

Snakes (novel)

The Song Turning Back into Itself (poems)

Who Is Angelina? (novel)

Geography of the Near East (poems)

Sitting Pretty (novel)

Ask Me Now (novel)

Bodies & Soul (musical memoirs)

The Blues Don't Change: New and Selected Poems

Kinds of Blue (musical memoirs)

Things Ain't What They Used to Be (musical memoirs)

Seduction By Light (novel)

Mingus Mingus: Two Memoirs (with Janet Coleman)

Heaven: Collected Poems 1956-1990

Straight No Chaser (poetry chapbook)

Drowning in the Sea of Love (musical memoirs)

*African American Literature:
A Brief Introduction and Anthology*
(textbook)

Conjugal Visits (poetry chapbook)

The Literature of California (anthology)
with Jack Hicks, James D. Houston,
and Maxine Hong Kingston

THE SOUND OF DREAMS REMEMBERED

Poems 1990-2000

Al Young

Illustrations by
Vivian Torrence

A Donald S. Ellis Book

Creative Arts Book Company
Berkeley

Some of these poems, in slightly different form, have already appeared in the fol-
lowing publications whose editors are thanked:

A Gathering of the Tribes (Steve Cannon), *Asili: The Journal of Multicultual
HeartSpeak* (Joseph P. McNair, Miami-Dade Community College), *Bombay Gin*
(Anne Waldeman; the Jack Kerouac School of Disembodied Poetics), *Brilliant
Corners* (Sascha Feinstein), *The Haight Ashbury Review* (Conyus Calhoun), *Konch*
(Ishmael Reed), *Mankato Foetry Review* (Roger Sheffer), *Michigan Quarterly
Review* (Laurence Goldstein), *Ploughshares* (Stories and Poems edited by Stuart
Dybek & Jane Hirshfield), *Poetry at the 33 Review* (Nancy Keane), *Quarterly
Journal of Ideology: A Critique of Conventional Wisdom* (Louisiana State University
in Shreveport; Dorie LaRue, poetry editor), *The San Diego Reader* (Judith Moore),
Seattle Review (Colleen J. McElroy), *Some Say Tomato* (the "Tomato" anthology
edited by Mariflo Stephens, Northwood Press), *The Southern California Anthology*
(Vol. XII; James Ragan, Sophia Nardin, and David Dorton; Master of Professional
Writing Program, University of Southern California, Los Angeles), *The Writing
Path 2: Foetry and Frose from Writers' Conferences* (Michael Pettit; University of
Iowa Press), *What Book!?: Buddha Foems from Beat to HipHop* (Gary Gach), *Wild
Duck Review* (Casey Walker).

Sally Swisher's lyric for the Thelonious Monk instrumental, "Straight No Chaser,"
is published under the title "Get It Straight"; copyright © 1988 by Sally Swisher
and BMG Music; transcribed from the album, *Carmen Sings Monk*, by Carmen
McRae (Novus CD 3086-2-N).

Coleman Barks translated the line, "There is no ahead"; penned by Rumi, extraor-
dinary 13th century Perisan poet (from *The Essential Rumi;* copyright © 1997 by
Coleman Barks).

"Sonnet #23" ("A thought within a thought within a thought") by Gladys
Schmitt; from *Sonnets for An Analyst* (Harcourt Brace Jovanovich, Inc.); copyright
© 1973 by the Estate of Gladys Schmitt.

Cover Art: Vivian Torrence, *Moments Are Feathers*, 2000

ISBN 0-88739-373-X
Library of Congress Catalog Number XX-XXXXXX

Printed in the United States of America

In memory of Ann K. Hinkel
(1909-1999),
teacher, spirit, and friend

"Love is a shoestring.
Any way you tie it, it may come undone.
Life is a new thing.
Every day something lost, something won."

—Billy Strayhorn
("Maybe")

"Work like you don't need the money.
Love like you've never been hurt.
Dance like nobody's watching."

—Leroy Robert "Satchel" Paige

Contents

THE SOUND OF DREAMS REMEMBERED

CONJUGAL VISITS

STRAIGHT NO CHASER

THE SOUND OF DREAMS REMEMBERED

APRIL IN PARIS

after Yip Harburg & Vernon Duke

It was here in that one-time, one-stop, lighted blue
of Paris at ease, close to the Cluny, in splendid,
straight-up noontime shadow that your slow and
measuring eyes met more than their burning match.

The smooth warmth of your whisper along my neck,
the nappy back of it, where you'd peeled back
its soft, excited collar to tell me everything you'd learned
or discerned in a city where love and prices flirt.

A product of standstill winters, sudden summers, sultry
prejudice, and heartland steak-and-whiskey afternoons,
you'd blown in from the States, an orphan of the arts—
Mary Cassatt, Josephine Baker, Mary Lou Williams,

Jean Seberg. What breathlessness overtakes me here?
Brushing and combing out memories of your touch,
in a season as uncertain as coastal fog moving inland
from the loveless edges of that country we'd both fled,

I shiver. Whom could we run to if not one another?
Back home we knew what it was like to be the other—
displaced, despised, imprisonable. We watched and fought.
The colors of loss deepened. Yearning to break free,

unconsciously American, we counted our chickens, certain
that the ships we'd always banked on would sail in.
In Paris, our adopted country of each other's arms,
whose borders blurred all time, all common market sense,

we saved the slow but steady squeeze of night, of time;
the way it smothered darkness, the way it mothered light.
The April of your frightened French was like that, too;
you had no words for holiday tables, for chestnuts in bloom.

Parisian light, like light at home—Detroit, Des Moines—
lit up your waifish eyes. I said, "Think twice before you speak."
Over here you mostly knew the blues; *rue* rhymed with blue.
There couldn't be too much light, or too much touch.

A POEM FOR LISTENERS

If, uplifting those fanning ears, the elephant
can hear ultra high frequency mating
calls placed from miles beyond this deafening sky,
then why can't sultry laughter like yours—
all piquancy and sass—take off? The rumble of it
sometimes makes its way to parts of me I long
to tour but haven't. In shining ring within ring,
the satellite brightness of your laughter lights heaven
at hand, out-circling itself like a rock dropped into a pond.
If Ravi Shankar could hear the gouache of anguish
washing through St. Coltrane's cries, or if Ravel could hear
the Gypsy strains of Spain that ruffled his composure
a borderline away, or if bats can hear the sound
of fruit flies walking, and if every city makes and leaves
its own soundprint, then, tell me, with your next hard laugh,
what animal ancestor of ours flowered in the sound of the note
the chord never needs to round itself out, but takes in
—thankful. Unpack, relax, and I'll tell you another one.

DESERT FOOTAGE: Three Dissolves

Egypt, Israel, Falestine & Arizona—
all in one heady spring season

1/

Crossing, we arrive, we change up, we come back
inside the original oasis, that quivering water, its
cool-holed message no mirage; a power-mirror. Ours.

2/

Brushes with sages, lifetime leads, unload, unjam
right here, where now don't need no start, don't need
no count; where lust, like dusty first-impressions, suns
up, suns down & falls away by twists & blazing turns.

Stopped cold by night, excitement slows. Zigzag,
the jazz of cactus fuzz & insect buzz & lizards whizzing
every whichway nowhere & buzzards minding their own
lazy business zooms, the horizon a shining rim-shot.

3/

Bowled over by blue, by light & cooling cloud, desert
can reach its peaks & depths, its flats & sharps,
with singular, insular pleasure. And treasures
we always haul back lack the track-record market value
wealth-wish we've been air-conditioned to cherish.

In malls & designer back alleys of urgent dreaming,
desire grinds & bumps & tallies & bills. But back here
at home, back smack in the desert, silence & space
ease in & replace get-&-gimme, mucho & gotcha.
Or is it we who get erased? The thrill of peace enthrones
out here, where water walks & kings don't mean a thing.

SANTA MONICA 1996

Having the Pacific right out the window works.
Melinda arrives in ten minutes. I'm out of breath,
out of everything you can never think of here where
women in a painting photo 1950 grace my wall
the way the Princess graced Monaco. They're all over
the beach, the sands, which seem to whisper: *"Shhh,*
we got us a white thing going down here in Southern Cal,
the official Southern California of oceanwear and depth.
The sea is as close and as deep to us as we need it to be."
Under the spell of sleeplessness, under the sun of night,
I fall awake. In this unwanted wakefulness I return
to God to go for broke. There seems to be no other choice.
The voice that reaches me has no wilderness connected
to it, no ventriloquial throw-out this song that speaks
to every particle in my body still in need. The light
guiding my surprise for all this time stays on.
In two weeks time can turn itself around and open me
again to the sound the Pacific makes now, when it says:
"I'm right outside your window, wayward man.
Come breathe me in and out, then promenade until
the you-who-lagged-and-lingered changes on a dime."

CHOPS

for Stephen Henriques

Be it Havana, Savannah, Urbana, Atlanta—
restraint ain't never quite the same as paint;
you can rally spread it around, or lay it on,
which isn't the same as the laying on of hands
or putting the rubber to the road, or calling
off your dogs. Calling off the beat comes close.
So in those homeless afternoons where winos
and crackheads turn up to nap on benches, and
in back alley doorways, under park bushes, or
inside the ebb tide of daytime nightmares—
frozen, gone limp—intention and meaning count.
More than false affection doled out at 5.6% APR
in an April that by June will jump back to hard times,
the way you show and tell how you feel and do speaks.
Like you, whoever hears it will chop what they need,
slice it thick or thin, and sand or leave it painted.
By then you'll be so cool, the sound of that touch
will make your trembling hands reach for a brush.

24 March 1997
(after hearing Gonzalo Rubalcaba
live at Yoshi's, Oakland)

AN AMERICAN CHAMPION IN LOVE

for Lilly Benton

On borrowed time, she took another prize,
yet something held her back, breathed down her neck.
What slowed her breathing slept around her eyes,
their salty edges thickening where flecks

of reckless, juicy light rushed in. First-place
no longer met her need, her bigtime dream.
Dissolving, sliding, melted on her face,
even her dreams would scald her when they steamed

into their hot half-lives, and she could feel
their weight, her medals. Wild sweat clogged her nose.
What had her on the run, what made her heel
and toe the line now? Love: the way it rose

like afternoon—no night before, no dawn,
no morning sun, no warning light, no clue.
Was it OK to cry, all right to yawn?
No frame of reference, no Things To Do

list ate at her. No, nothing but a glimpse
of parted clouds remembered; skydive gear,
the rush a silly monkey's jump, a chimp's;
the moving ground a grin from ear to ear.

Fear suited up; love cut her gut some slack.
To run only to win seemed pointless, dumb—
like living on the mark. Get set! Attack!
Where had the old thrill gone? Now she felt numb;

she'd lost her heart, but how? No silver cup,
no bronze, no plaque, no cash, no ribbon went
with territory wired to trip her up
at every turn. Tricky. What had win meant?

Where had she spent her childhood—in a vault?
She loved to run; her parents loved to win.
She'd win a race and turn a somersault
— and Daddy, Mommy, both would clap and spin.

Her trainers told her: "Stop that! Act your age,
be dignified. Don't pull that kinda stuff."
So, sure enough, she studied the sports page,
TV, news magazines, and even rough,

old, scratchy training films they showed at school:
the '36 Olympics in Berlin;
Ben Johnson's fall; why steroids were uncool—
that German girl they'd caught with doctored urine.

Routinely they watched re-runs of their meets
on videotape. What could they teach? Sometimes
her fantasies would beat their own retreats,
flickering with pissed-off Hitlers, busted rhymes

she'd hear and picture blasting while she raced.
When Wilma Rudolph cheered her from the stands,
she knew she couldn't lose; the meet was aced.
She'd dreamed of setting records, foreign lands,

Olympic sprinting, winning, triumph, cash.
Poor, sickly Wilma never told herself:
"A hundred-meter relay or a dash?
Two hundred? Hey, no way. I'm on the shelf

with this bad leg of mine. Just count me out."
So just as all her heroes had inspired
the way she outstepped shadows, undid doubt,
this runner always scored. She never tired,

never ran out of steam, or guts or balls,
whatever girls ran out of—ovaries?
A winner, yes, but not the kind who hauls
off, takes the cake, and splits. October sees

to that; her birthday month, a lucky time
of year. "I'm yours," October always told her.
"To crave my light has never been a crime."
A patriot she was; no athlete-soldier

dispatched to patch up social policies.
Democracy's a tyranny, she'd read
in Plato's *The Republic;* ancient Greece.
Their lit class gasped. What nerve! That's what he'd said.

We've got the greatest system in the world.
There never would've been a U.S.A.
if every king and queen and duke and earl
and emperor and tyrant had their way.

She'd fight for that, oh yes, she would defend
the land she loved, the only home she knew,
the same way Jesse Owens put an end
to Nazi big talk, proving who was who.

Her country? Love? Which would she sacrifice
when duty called, if push came down to shove?
The fix was in; she thought it rather nice
to let it hang, not have to choose—just love.

ANIMAL

That such an easing sound should make its moves
so smoothly on the tongue and in the flesh—
all padded paws, all cockatoos or hooves
—says something big about the ways we mesh.
Where once we granted soul its anima,
instinctively aware that raw volition
goes just so far (the same as stamina),
we worship bio-tech now; new religion.
The animal in ocean, jungle, stone—
we don't see with our eyes, but with our minds.
Intelligence, we think, is ours alone.
We smell, we groan, we pull our monkeyshines.
We speak and paint and dance and write and sing.
We snoop out landscapes where all bets are off,
where clothes stay packed and we, the King
and Queen of Soul, can do our stuff.
Maybe we love cartoons because they're us
except with anima put back in place.
These crazy ways we learn again to trust
the seal, the crocodile who wears our face.

WHO I AM IN TWILIGHT

Like John Lee Hooker, like Lightnin Hopkins,
like the blues himself, the trickster sonnet,
hoedown, the tango, the cante jondo,
like blessed spirituals and ragas custom-made,
like sagas, like stories, like slick, slow,
sly soliloquies sliding into dramas,
like *Crime & Punishment*, like death & birth,
Canal Street, New Orleans, like the easy,
erasable, troubled voices a whirling
ceiling fan makes in deep summer nights in
hot, unheavenly hotels—Oklahoma, Arkansas,
Tennessee—like the Mississippi River
so deep and wide you couldn't get a letter
to the other side, like Grand Canyon,
like Yosemite National Park, like beans &
cornbread, like rest & recreation, like love
and like, I know we last. I know our bleeding stops.

BLUE COLLAR NIGHT

In the window of her room at Motel 6, the regional
McDonald's accounts officer checked me out, summed up
and balanced all her figures when she saw my absurd array:
the bags and loads and worlds I was juggling on my way up.
Or was I headed down? Stairs were no measure.
The way she stared told stories, told me, told the world
how shaky I had grown in this spring of poor mutts,
excuses, and road kill. At Best Western they were hosting
the California Highway Patrol convention. "Are you C.H.P?"
the pert and proper sister asked. "Do I look like C.H.P.?"
Not really up to waiting out her answer, I remembered April,
its reputation for cruelty. OK, that's cool. The rest of you months,
you're on your own. If "Tough Shit" Eliot meant
what he wrote about the waste, then wasting, now wasted land,
then what went down in history as poetry-in-motion—
meaning: poems-on-the-the-fly—means even I, no Prufrock,
not by a long shot—may last through this sorry night.
Yes, *last*, my friend. Populism is almost the same as true religion.

**POEMS
CAIRO 1998**

1/

ONE PRAYER'S PRAYER AT SUNSET

Blue wail over the Nile under orange
sunfall spreads like a video signal,
like a binary zero to one, God to creation,
citywide, nationwide. Population: 1.
Well-tuned ears will recognize
the everlasting, catch-all thrill of worship
in a world self-willed to obscurity.

It is as if we turned blind eyes to the sun,
or deaf ears to the roar of traffic
inside of us where thoughts and feelings
race and rush and jam and collide
on clogged freeways to the soul.

Allahhhhh. Love like weather pours out
from within like weather unwatched but
in measure as right as Celsius, as Fahrenheit.
In calm degrees of faith and faithfulness.
the eye of all suns, the soul of all rivers smiles.
Nile. Sky. Light. Love. Salaam. Amin. Amin.

2/

MILKY LIGHT OF NIGHT

Milky light of night all oil along the Nile,
what stars, what moons have come to your rescue
time after time after time in this land of richness
and multitudes? When my darkened people sang,
"Tell old Pharoah, 'Let my people go,'" we were
going for broke, my friends. We were crying
from a wilderness that never got cleared.
Most of us knew only an Old Testament Egypt,

an Egypt of parchment, a colonialized kaleidescope
of wonders and signs. Few knew about Nubia,
about the "black *but* comely" clause planted
by King James' color-crazed translators in
The Song of Solomon. There was no "but" there
to pound beauty into sand; the right word was *ana.*
Here in this fertile light, on this motherly soil,
captor and captive, actor and activity connect.
Now when the Negro speaks of rivers, she will have
to explain more than the parting of the Red Sea;
she'll have to own the droughts, the floods, the Siwa
oasis in the desert: arrow and bow, Pharoah and Jew.

3/

IN ALEXANDRIA

> *"There lived in Alexandria*
> *In wicked Alexandria ..."*
> — "Thais," Anglo-American folk song

What happens to a dream deferred
through years of sleepy wakefulness,
through colorful comparisons
drawn up by writers long ago
who came and wrote their living wills?
Durrell, Kavafy, love in flames;
The Red Sea, rapture, Muslim, Jew,
Greek Orthodoxies in the name of
side by side we live our creeds,
fulfill love's needs; the light, the light,
the cornices, the sea a means
for dreaming big, what happens when
the market tours and gorgeous lures
get shot down cold? The histories,
the feel and sprawl and subtle call
of Alexandria drowned in time
comes back in fish and garlic, lime
lugged up one hour and downed the next.

What happens when warm tributes paid
to commerce, trade and tolerance
slow down, when chilling massacres
occur to slur the loveliness
of soulful legacies. What sun,
what sea can save a dream deferred?

What happens to a dream deferred
to sleeplessness?
Does it pester you
all day long, or does it stun
like the new Egyptian sun?

4/

SLEEPLESS IN EGYPT

for Inez

You be the judge, just prick yourself to see
what gives, what happens when you finally free
yourself from fears that you won't sleep at all;
that you'll be out cold when your wake-up call
gets placed. Your face feels frozen. Now the five
a.m. prayer cry zings through the live
air out your window, amplified and fresh,
from one alert old muezzin. Voices mesh;
the siren squad car whines of ambulance
or fire engine. Customized, horns dance
along the edge of time, its generous forms.
Ra actually turns up, drops in, sits and warms
the brightest pair of feet you've ever seen;
they're tiny, glowing, sweet, blue-lotus green.
You say, "Could you slip one shot of your bliss
into my veinless night? I need the kiss
of sleep? Please, just this once, one miracle?"
The Sun God says, "Asleep? Awake? Be clear. Recall
your origins, your journey overall;
commandments that I knew you'd never keep.
Then ask about the needlessness of sleep."

14

MONDO BONGO

Bad drumming always pounds out good,
but badder bongo builds and builds, abounds.
Your everlasting rhythmicness astounds
statues like us who've always understood
you got to get down, down, bippity-bippity down

CAT WHISPERS FROM THE BEYOND

in memory of joka

You watch me this way everyday alone
crouched like this, staring at the swimming pool.
And if you think of anything except
yourself, perhaps you've wondered what I see,
or what I think about, or feel, or know.
I know my time is short, and so I'll tell
you what I think's important to a cat.
There was a time when people worshipped us,
when magic powers were ours for mere meows.
Though cats still feel in style, the rage has cooled
enough to throw the backdoor open for pigs
to roll in, pet rocks, crickets, Furbees; worse.
If you would know my thoughts, bring a flashlight.
The territory makes this darkness rush
straight, head-on at you like, well, like real life.
Some hang in yupped up cybernet cafés,
steamed milk or cappuccino close at hand;
I hang here by the pool, a furry fool
sidetracked by love and by reflection. Ugh!
But you don't see no scrimmage taking place;
there's no Narcissus here, no image drowned.
I'm still just me, just plain old who-I-am.

STEP OUT ON THE TIGHTROPE AND DON'T LOOK DOWN

> *"Each time I play, I step out on*
> *the tightrope and don't look down."*
> —Marian McPartland

There were problems, problems, problems, and she had them
almost down. Mastering the languages of daylight helped
her make it through the night, 98.6 percent. Tunisia didn't count.
She didn't think she could write melody, only arrangements—
or so she thought. It was largely personal, hugely undigital.
How do you carve an elephant out of a block of granite?
You get rid of all the parts that aren't an elephant.
And so in the days when music wasn't everywhere, she sat in
a little joint where she could drink coffee and nosh.
She scribbled one dozen poems in one night, each one a classic;
each designated, destined to be anthology fodder. Set to music,
two turned into hits for singers who, like her, worked best
without a net. Big money, big problems; big problems, big dookey
whizzed in and she grabbed at them the way a high wire
artist might grab at a hot wire on no notice, no nod, no notion
of what lies ahead. Seen clearly, daylight moved back in
and problems blacked out into their blameless blue origins.
"Once again," she told the press, "I bow to the Muse."
Was her Muse the blues? How many falses? How many trues?

THE AMERICANIZATION OF SOLITUDE

A blaring afternoon obeys no law.
The jailing scream of it—American.
No sky looks Afro-blue through bars or mesh.
No solitude or quietude enjoys
itself. Detained or caged, bad music plays
unfairly with the soul. Sound stabs and wounds.

All small, remaining joys get jammed against
the hard, loud odds plea-bargaining affords.
"Couldn't you turn it down a little bit?"
You argue this politely, confident
that reason cools, that common sense will out.
But, no, it's you who gets impounded, pal.

Where silence isn't welcomed, it becomes
a knife sharp at the throat, a gun to head
off threatening intruders like the blues
of thought; the sound of being with yourself.
Dictatorship, hands down, feels digital.
No shores, no oceans, thank you, U.S.A.

CRICKET TALK

In the night at dead center
life comes to itself—alive and
shifting with every chirp
and dog bark; evening a smoothing,
early night the nut and bolt of time turning
at heaven's gate: the soul.

Free this sibilant bedding of solitude
one mood at a time. When tickets
get sold to cricket-shows, I'll be the first
to go. What lonely, lonely nights
these admissions will buy
on any planet, together or alone
with your chirping, longing self;
the sounds of one mind transmitting,
receiving—thinking just doesn't tell
the story somehow. Electrical laughter.
Cricket talk.

DREAMING A RENOIR IN LONDON

In a slow morning dream that played before
that damn crack of dawn hammering began
across the garden, I chose a particular orange
from a particular dish and, wishing its taste
into my dozing, eager mouth, I peeled and
pulled, inhaling thin-skinned mists until
its fruity will broke in tender surrender.

The sheer divinity of this suspension owes
as much to *Star Trek* as it does to medieval
paintings in which we look at the heads of angels
and virgins enclosed in luminous globes of light.
The orange, plucked from a dream-bowl colored
up by Pierre-Auguste Renoir in another country,
in another century, rolled into the sleepy fold
of desire all curled and ready to receive.

French, the disguised counterwoman, her hair
as dark as all the backgrounds of my dreams,
knew how my yawning yearned for a sweetness
that would always be under construction;
the taste of touching, the fragrant look of silence.

FAITH

Like a clear stream that forever runs,
like the highway, freeways, main arteries
which are in truth rivers, faith flows.
What's there to think about? Click.
At the flip of a switch, the tap of a button,
lights come on, whole global engines gyrate
almost noiselessly; electrons move and point
in perfectly correct directions—faith.

Mash on a floor and there's the rug, the earth,
that rolling river again underneath, intimate
as blood, which flows as breath, which flows,
as everything alive must ebb and flow.
Whom should we think the flowing has to stop?
Knowing knows it knows. Or better: Faith trusts
and needs itself more than anything faith thinks
it needs to believe to stay alive.

But when faith thinks or, worse, when faith explains,
watch out. To move out of the rain, but run
heels over head into the sea—what is the point?
To know exactly when to fall asleep
without a single hint from anyone—faith.
If that's the way it works, it works.
With living surety, time moves in time
and out of time through time zones so fluently
we barely know to catch more than a moment.

Faith knows how to imagine what's timeless
by what is timed. Faith carries the sun
inside itself and shines it out in the dark.

DÉTROIT MOI

I

Who says the autumn sonata is not the loveliest of all?
In ancient Detroit, French exploiters like Antoine de la Mothe
Sieur de Cadillac and the generous Father Richard knew

the meaning of Rolling on the River centuries before
Creedence Clearwater hunked it out. When October rain came
to Lake Ponchartrain, O how Great Lakes winds blew cold

across and bowed the strings of a Stradivarius, hushed, blasé!
Cadillac knew he didn't have much time to sweat it;
his big gig as Governor of Louisiana was coming up.

The fix was in. To hell with all the wild pigs out there
uprooting Belle Isle! Nobody knew the trouble they'd see.
Nobody knew how ruthlessly the troublesome Negroes

would migrate, would move Louisiana, Texas, Arkansas,
Mississippi, chicken bones, spare ribs and all, straight up
to Michigan. And with them—packed, billed out and bound to go

—your red and white and blue people, your purple mountain
majesty people, some fruitfully, some truthfully plain.
O Lady Be Good. And the Lady of Our profit, she was good.

The Cream of Michigan Café, 12th Street, its prehistoric
gleam distilled with raw gangster moonlight in the pull-down
Purple Gang nights, sang her virtues. This was Jewish splendor,

this was life that came down heavily on the side of live
(as in give and let give, get and let get). Friends and lovers
in the dharma, how easy it is to forget that every mouth

you twitch to kiss, each cheek you speak your half of stories to,
and every body you long to hold magnificently belongs

to someone nestled in the somewhere they come from.

They return in dreams, in daydreams, in the ways they walk
or worry, hold their mouths, or gaze across a ruined café, or smoke.
Those many somewheres do not sit alone; their someones leave

to start new families by design, or on the fly. A song,
a rhapsody, a blacked-out blues, a softening autumn sonata
can take you up to Canada and back, the watery crawl a cry away.

The emigré who danced or listened hard to dreams escaped.
Endurance wasn't measured by the mapped rabbit's leap
above glove, but by which peninsula of Michigan you reached.

II.

Autumn sonata. 1937. When Henry Ford sent a payroll of goons
to break the union ties, to crack the onion heads of strikers
and their ilk, the rusting stream of red at River Rouge grew thick.

All down between the cracks, all up and down, the earth was bled.
Gone Russia shone with blood. Brown shirts were turning black.
Back in Detroit the car to be somebody in became a Cadillac.

So Ferdinand Destouches, the doctor-writer, sailed into Big D. as Céline.
Now we know there was a woman involved, a nurse, no, a Detroiter
who ended up becoming his obsession. By profession, the Nazi

strain of things unlinked and let this solid block of properties become
the Arsenal of Democracy. If the Czechs construct their Monument
to the Victims of Communism, someone will have to build another:

Monument to the Victims of Capitalism. Bohunks of the world, unite!
You have nothing to lose but your tedious prejudices. When they ask
and you can't identify hometowns of colorful Americans, say Detroit.

Say Robert Hayden, Lily Tomlin, Gladys Knight, Madonna,
Marge Piercy, Mitch Ryder, Philip Levine, Diana Ross, Joe Henderson,
Marvin Gaye, Elmore Leonard, Aretha Franklin, Michael Moore,

Alice Coltrane, Joyce Carol Oates, Dan I. Slobin, Toi Derricotte,
David Wellman, Andrei Codrescu, Danny Thomas, Lee Iacocca,
Gerry Mulligan, Donald Byrd, Hank and Thad and Elvin Jones,

Smokey Robinson, Malcolm X, Lawrence Joseph, Barry Harris,
Paul Chambers, John Sinclair, Yusef Lateef, Stevie Wonder—
and if your blue sonata thrills like Detroit in the fall, call Al Young.

FOR MS. PC MACK, MY LANGUAGE POET PAL

> *"Given the choice of seeing a lantern-show*
> *about Heaven and going to Heaven, most*
> *Americans would choose the lantern-show."*
> —attributed to Oscar Wilde

1/

And that's the case on this plane
right now where flight attendants
just told the whole plane to pull down
its window shades and turn off its lights,
and most have done just that.
I stick around, typing in code.

There are ways to get into this slowly
and without crisps or milk to attract competition.
There are ways to go to heaven undercover.

2/

The impossibility of working this way
suggests I shift at once into numbers, and
maybe keep it that way until the story can be
told in old-fashioned digits: the fingers
of two hands, two toes perhaps, where you will
one day be able to avoid electronic detection
altogether. Only don't count on it.
In this contrabasso world of strange opinions
and equipment to back it up, numbers count
more than ideas or principles or light.
Spread across the breadth of an Argentine asada
(barbecue to you, achoo!), the tango hears us now.

POETRY AND PUBLIC POLITICS

Poetry not so much invades as makes
public space that winter cannot cut without icing
everything over and up. Out don't count.

It ain't no piece of cake, but you ain't got to call
no 911, either. When all is said and done,
when morning blows coolly through your bedroom window,
slatting your face with shadows of mini-blinds,
art knows more than you know now about cook-offs,

write-offs and change. Because you still loathe capitalism,
you hunger; you cheat yourself. You've passed up sound,
exotic boodie. You've missed out on some good food, too.

Baby, maybe like exquisite air-dried cheese, the luxury
of spirit weakens. Time keeps no record. You age.
Life mellows, then explodes to the taste like silence.

You love it. You love life's golden imperfections,
your democratic exclusion from key events, the polls;
this phase of moon you see, campaign and care for.

SUNDAYS IN DEMOCRACIES

for Peter Zimmels

Republicans: You're poor because
you're ignorant of all the laws
our Congress passed to cut the costs
of schooling children who get tossed,
nay, dumped upon society.
While we do view with piety
the right to life, we draw the line.
Clean up your act. To woo or wine
the loser class does not make sense.
Let's get this straight. We never winced
at taking public time to quarrel
with victims, thugs, the huge immoral
segment of the population
in our great, God-blessed, rich, free nation.

The Democrats: There was a time
the GOP and all its crime
got barely covered by the news,
which only aired *our* sins and blues.
What have they done for you, my friends?
Is making do or making ends
meet any measure of success?
We back the same Big Business mess
they do, but when we tighten your belt
we dig up Franklin Roosevelt.
We've given you prosperity
without their stark severity.
The only thing we have to fear?—
Republicans. Now, is that clear?

A Citizen: More parties, please,
more Sundays in democracies!
Each party dances, each side sings;
one great Big Bird with two right wings.

They'll boogie with you in the streets,
then drag you down to dark defeats.
Democracy? Look at our heroes:
CEO's billions, labor's zeroes—
pure DNA, unspliced and spliced.
If you think oil is over-priced,
consider what we're going to pay
for giving frequencies away—
the broadcast band. I say let's vote.
Let's kick some butt, let's rock some boat.

FILMING

Another side show while the camera rolls
unfolds along the edges. One close look
at what's not shot, but focused on the cast,
and she saw stars. The realm of film unfolds.

She sees the ways she didn't look at him.
She sees all mirrors opening to the soul.
UCLA could take the credit for
a lot of this—say, everything but them.

She wanted stardom badly. She could taste
its swirl, its slippery feel slide down her throat.
Hot lights, soft nights, directors yelling "Cut!"
Why darkness? Why let beauty go to waste?

The biggest thrill of all just might have been
that side show mirrored; by her own self seen.

CÓRDOBA

for Christina

The huge allure of you out of control—
it crazes, glazes me; it's just too hard
sometimes. Was this what they called rock and roll?
When you won't give an inch, I take a yard.

I claim whole regions of your love: the east,
the coast, the plains and, yes, the south.
Of course the you who smoothly calms the beast
in me, I love her, too. I put my mouth
to hers sometimes just to resuscitate
that ancient spirit-feel; to re-connect.
Holed up inside her, though, I find you. Bait-
and-switch: a trick I've tracked, but don't expect.
Huge, out of focus, rushing edges, shores,
we plunge. Imagine Spain. Imagine Moors.

LANDSCAPE MODE

Overlooking the Cumberland River,
Clarksville, Tennessee,
early November 1996

In ancient Chinese paintings we see more sky than
earth, so when clouds hurry by in silver-gray
inkbursts of rolling readiness right along the river,

ripe with rain, rushing the road of time along,
pushing back light, belittling the black and white clarity
of Hollywood in its prime, the eye climbs down to greet

with shining gusto trees along the shore. Opryland
beyond the frame, the blue horizon hidden in a sea
of possibilities. And beyond this there's jazz: Jimmy Giuffre's

"Train on the River" stretched out strong like a pet cat
—and that's that. But not quite. This poem paints
poorly what sketchers and colorists do best. The rest

should come out empty, allowing you to fill in your own
basic emptiness, your openness, your self-portrait
forged and catalogued; on quiet exhibit, on temporary loan.

Descended from clouds immensely more ancient than China,
you never quit becoming the background, the field in a sky
whose eubtle earthiness sails over our heads altogether.

LA MICHICANA

"Why do you even keep the same phone number?"
asked Terri Juarez, wanting to feel perhaps the soft wind
of Florida keying her blues and making the sun shake
where it rose inside her risen windows like
some last fair deal going down. The key of course
was pitched to catch your ear, then warble and fade.
And when you thought about the madness of Cubans
in Miami wanting Elián Gonzáles to reject his father,
reject his motherland, reject himself and he's only a kid,
you knew how crazy the whole world had become
and you, suddenly a breaker of hearts, did not answer.
You did not know how to say: "Terri, *guapa*, Terri, baby,
never did I not wish to hear from you; I only hoped
you would one day quit screaming into the phone
in the middle of some nights when the Aztec, the Cuban,
the Yoruba prayer or proverb I needed made you
seem like the Michicana you were, a Tejana wannabe."
From Michigan to Texas to Florida you'd rambled,
slumbering through lifetimes, putting up with love.

HOW BEAUTY PEEKS AT YOU

Human conditioning feels nothing like air
conditioning: that fierce arctic smile.
The true trailway to yellowness
blazed by sun, the moon follows
on little not yet colt feet. This is eternity;
this is the way oceans form themselves
under seemingly no supervision but love's.

Summer: the perfect maturation.
Winter keeps, and spring miscegenates
(bad grass, good hair), but fall delivers
everytime; perfects October. Deep-down,
the reddening of the forest testifies.
God's glory—never stolen, never stumped
—lies at the center of its own; splendid, shy.

POEM IN JANUARY

Late thoughts must push
through clouds of reckoning.
The you who moves from a town
50 miles from where you lived once,
maybe twice, maybe all
your precious life will change.
You'll float perhaps; you'll surely be
seduced by change herself.
And if September never comes
on time, you'll understand.
The perfect cure for all that ails
feels right around some corner;
the turn you're just about to take.
Better late than wait a nanosecond
longer. Gradual change chews;
sudden change consolidates.

LOVE POEM

Sometimes, like an ocean whose motion
taps into moon power alone, you turn to me.

With earlobes and eyes, mouth and nose;
with heat-seeking arms you surround me,

and with a wild silence you tell me things
you never would or could have known alone.

Yes, you, the oscillating, wave-like friend
of the world whose particles have traveled

so inevitably towards mine that sometimes
the moon forgets its moves, and the sea,

well, sometimes seas can be the last to grasp
what's finally going on. What goes on here,

in this house, in this heart, in this inexhaustible art
that ranks right up there with taxes, death and

time, is (how else to save, how else to put it) love.
I wade into an ocean-you, pulled and lulled by love.

SAMPLER

Poems occur; they don't get written.
If a mango hits you smack in the face in
the marketplace, Lima, chalk it up to Peru
and some hooligan spirit gone amok.
Love operates that way, too. Love says:
"Look, it's been a long, long time since
I've come up against an ornery non-believer like you,
but I'm going to come clean and treat you
as if you've gone along with me all along, OK?"
And there in the kitchen of your memory,
cues will guide you concisely and precisely
all the way back to subtle, sly kinds of lyrics and
cuisines you loved and specialized in as soon as
trade routes of the Middle Ages brought new foods
to the table, to the palate where new tastes were painted.
There, right there in the midst of your retrieved psyche,
love giggles in ways no gaggle of geese can match.
In other worlds, the pure food of you thrives,
nurturing friend and foe alike; feeding even
the skeletons in your closet, feeding their lions,
crossing every barrier but the ones you erect.
And if from Lima you journey to Rio to pay tribute
to the memory of Antonio Carlos Jobim, relax
and sample the sunlit laughter and horror of
that fabulous city on fire with rhythm and a blues
the power of Macumba itself studies before it steps in.
And when you write it down, let go and watch
what happens and goes on happening era after era
after era. Sample the sea that salts your spirit.

IN TWO'S

New ways to make love old feel more than right.
Always the mighty, heady rush of light

from one side of the sky clean to the next
clears air, clears minds, clears room for lazy sex

to sprawl. You all know how this deal comes down.
Chilean general and corporate clown

alike will stand trial for their haughty crimes
in these, the best, the worst; the blankest times

of all. When was the last time you cried foul?
Are you the sparrow, or are you the owl?

JACUZZI JAZZ

for Al "Hassan" Wardlow

Hassan, you're right about the thing they like—
it's jazz, the word. That's it all right. And then?
Sometimes you have to coolly steel or psych
yourself to not remember Clifford, Ben,
or Monk. Those nights the heart would break in two
unless you fixed on Griffin, Sarah, Max;
an afternoon in Paris, J.J. blue
enough to burn big holes and drool wet tracks
for Stitt to sand and dry and polish raw.
So where you're coming from, and where the smart
young MBA's and MFA's would draw
the line between Jazz Is, Jazz Ain't, take heart—
it's just as moldy figs and snobs suspect:
the lines don't necessarily intersect.

32

EINE KLEINE NACHTMUSIK,
(or, THE DOCTOR AFTER HOURS)

Her tones: bones heard and graphed;
audible like the cricket regularity
of hushed and muffled champagne talk.

She rests inside your skin, barely
understandable, yet ancient, complete;
ancient, atonal (no Shoenberg but, rather,

Vivaldi in Winter or Jimi Hendrix
unfurling his own spangled banner),
her every line a whine. Laughter

rarely registers on her stethoscope
the way death and loneliness do.
She needs and needs to laugh and laugh.

She needs someone six foot tall or
not there at all to cry and cry and cry with;
somebody with a soft, deep voice

to read aloud the Hemlock Society brochure
to patients more patient than she can become.
Kicked back, the doctor is definitely out.

IN FLIGHT

More, far more, than skin deep, beauty runs
gamuts, man. It can make up for lots of faults,
for plenty of blemishes, yet beauty can't pass
for what it is not. Equipped, it lasts and stays.

The view of Greenland from a rear window
on a trip to Frankfurt, connecting to Cairo,
beautifies the night of baby cries
and misbegotten restlessness. Yes,
scientists may have found their water
on the moon. But imagining lunar ice
underground seems no match for Greenland-
turning-Iceland in front of our island eyes.

"The white man," a womanly elder declares,
"is fixing to leave here and move to the moon.
Fixing to leave all these Negroes and Mexicans and
Chinese and A-rabs and things down here on Earth,
now that he's messed it up with all this pollution
and poison." Easy to see, her words are hard
to prove. Mineral rights. Eminent domain—
the catch-words crash upon the ear.

But beauty, my friend, upon which a visible glow
warms and brightens, the curvature of Earth,
the skin of space around the body—that is
a range; distances immeasurably blue-and-green blooded.

The religion of beauty and the science of knowing
drift like ice floes into one another along curves
so stunning that the skin that houses our pulsing
and exquisitely timed bloodworks still
wonders if who made the lamb made good.

THE SKIN OF LIGHT

To fill a room, a space, a vacuum
unattended without coming apart. A part
of your container, light plays and works like that.

In darkest Michigan, light fizzles in December long
before noon. The sun and moon of it hangs out
on precipices thin enough to slice, where steam meets ice.

What "light deprivation" relieves—who loves
to know? The garish sun of Southern Cal feels
like a dream to Hoosiers or Maine's downeasterners.

Light makes up forms that emptiness assumes.
"Form follows function," said the famous 19th century
architect whose name we wear so lightly memory fades.

To this, light itself might add: "And function follows
focus; pointed, star-like. Do not take lightly the miracle
of light; the shiny play of time and time and time.

That light can travel billions of its years to reach
our sleepy eyes proves how this all fits: O see
as light the field upon which we earn our blazing points.

JUST A FLAT-FOOTED LONDON SINGER

for joan Merrili

Jazz, what were you supposed to be?
I'm not that woman at the microphone,
gardenia scented from habits older
than and bolder than time. Time is a thief,
sayeth Kurt Weill, speaking you.

How California spoils and spills over
into the simply complex Billie songs
of a lovely Marin County afternoon
emphatically post-London. Lotte Lenya?
Did you hear what just got said

in British to perfectly match your German-
smart American English? Chilly but rarely
foggy these days, London bristles, London
bridges brag, and London walks me home.
I'm not that woman at the mike, but sing

I still can do. "A Foggy Day," no, but
weather—thick and wet, unsilhouetting—
works. Scotland knows; the Irish coast
surely. The London loving me was always
furry with cloud, comfortered with it

and smoky in the cigarette permissiveness
of my European unions. Like Etta Jones,
I never was much for shaking my shoulders
to signify this, or raising my eyebrows
to signal that. I'm just a flat-footed London singer.

SPONTANEOUS COMBUSTIBLES
(Languages of the American Southwest)

Air can burn oxygen when it speaks
everyday languages of the Southwest:
Xochimilco, Mexico, Coca Cola, Texaco—
"Ey, amigo, ¿cómo estás?" "Just don't try
to bring anything into the security area, OK?"
Who knows what code they're keeping
when they scoop their coins from the phone
slot, or when they say, "Se salen más que
los internacionales"? Barcelona, Bombay, Cairo.
Or "Nasty! Those were the nastiest stewardesses
I've ever seen"? "How nasty were they?"
"Take my word, they was nasty. They had
strings of spit hangin from they mouth,
they had make-up all graped up in they eyes.
O they was nasty!" Talk can get nasty, too.
In those hard cases, where spit flies, where
no-counts spout no content, talk will not ask
no cover charge. Big deserts, who thrive
in the silence that slices their sullen hot light,
speak out in languages we see more than hear,
feel more than smell, get more grasp. Understanding,
then, when it breaks into flame, breaks hearts
open. Caloric by nature, heat flowers by feeding
on itself. Drawn to a drowsy lingo that yawns
when it could gasp, nods when it could wink,
and naps when it could disappear, air burns
the time curved up inside of it, mixed up with it,
with the perfect beauty of loud, dumb talk.

SWEET BLOOD CALL

The holy powers of ghosts are such
that you might find yourself with light,
with child; immaculate, the old you

altered, new. Where your late blood
(once rusted, thrice wild) used to flow
out beyond the pull of all tides, you tick.

Against all odds, you pray, call out;
you ask and get. For this umbilical kiss,
all fast-forward future geneticists will kill.

POEM WITH MONICA LEWINSKY & BILL CLINTON

We the People, have the right to know, they say, but, hey—
know what? Know this: that when what happens comes down
down and dirty, it comes down hard on the side of big.
Hopelessness becomes a soap, and happenstance, a dance.

To the maul and mash of media speed, the need to know
gets needled into veins no blood counts on to last. Big hits
rock back on the heels of real hurricanes, real overthrows, real
profits and predictions. At CNN, at Fox and Westinghouse;

at MS-NBC, at ABC; at-large the panic spreads with ease.
Disease of course is never mentioned here. No doctor spins
the meaning of headline addiction: a superimposition,
cult-like, clueless, under-classed, and under glass. The pins

from Port au Prince we saw shut down a London café cold.
Under the T.S. Eliot Bridge on the other side of the Thames,
the Wasteland, out there where the Isle of Dogs barks
hard and hardly, we lay. Incautiously, all ears shut down.

Any good editor would tell her author: "You've got to make it
believable! What President would call a war to man-handle
a scandal? When nothing else works, wag. Plunk down
your magic card. We take no prisoners. Period. The End."

Who knows? Apologize. With "We the People" you could
lose your touch. Your grip: slippery, slow, a slump.
Sometimes you want and need to give the story its glory.
They might have even loved each other. What do we know?

RUSH

She missed the lavish hush and swish,
the cool, safe sound of leaves on trees
in streets where they'd been rich.
She missed the festive breeze
fame swept her up in. No costly drink,
no posh cuisine could even hold a candle
to the thrill of trembling on the brink
of sudden stardom, a bitch to handle.
Granted. But she'd loved it. Bigtime.

She missed their flashy swimming pool;
its drop-dead size and shape, the climb
back out, the diving in, the warming jewel-
like look of light across the tiles.
She missed it all: the deals, the studio calls,
make-up, shoots, interviews, the hype. Files
of clippings, fan mail, scripts, her dizzy walls
lonely with snapshots, big posters in French,
Italian, Polish, Japanese—cold keepsakes,
maybe, but they laid it out. Inch by inch
they proved she'd won the only sweepstakes
that count. She'd done it twice in this icy
town where, win or lose, just don't you miss the boat.

The killing cost of what she missed (pricey
barely said it), even that didn't float
far in her shoreless sea of gut-deep blues.
She missed the in-your-face power-rush
reality of celebrity. And she would choose
those streets again; the swish, the loving hush.

THE GOLD RUSH REVISITED

The gold rush as panacea, a way; the DNA
to wind and wrap around the dream. Mummified,
you ask: "How is the dream connected to real life?"
Driving it home this morning, freeway-locked,
high winds blew you this way and that and made it hard
to navigate. Twice you had to pull off to the side
and rest there, waiting for the *Grapes of Wrath*
effects to simmer down. Love, where whenever
I need you do you flee? Don't tell me bright
young parents can't make ends meet without stock
options, initial public offerings, a monster house, a Lexus,
$20 mil. Entitlement and world survival do not mesh
with suitcase dreams of cash and rocket stock.
Where aerospace once made the deals unreel;
now it's all cyberspace, all up for grabs, all silly con.
That we no longer sell a good or service we can touch
but spin, inflate and pump and float and digitize,
then dump, go public, and leap before we look
must mean: Put everything you got into death.
Life doesn't pay off. The rush to be rich is what counts.

THE REAL BIRD WORLD

The minute she said it,
  that sharp little girl,
that I couldn't make it
  in the real bird world;

the instant the words
  flew out of her mouth,
Florida came to me,
  anyplace south—

Phoenix, Los Angeles,
  Cuba, Peru
("Nah," said some other voice,
  "Cuba won't do").

On the Peninsula,
  here by the Bay,
pigeons and seagulls
  keep out of my way.

They stay out of my way,
  I stay out of theirs,
but there's just no escaping
  dumb comments and stares

that people throw at me;
  the least of my needs.
The bullshit I've fathomed
  —at high and low speeds!

The household I lived in
  didn't know when to quit—
the TV, the boombox,
  the hours they'd sit

talking crap on the cordless,
  or printing out stuff.
The chitchat, the racket!
  Too much was enough.

So how crazy were they?
  Well, that's hard to gauge.
Not one of them thought about
  me in that cage.

Last week they unlocked it,
  their pager went "Beep!"
I cleared the Dutch door
  without making a peep.

I may not last out here.
  You know how it is.
But I did have the sense
  to get out of showbiz.

THE PLUM SOFA

Nights of nights of filament by filament reliving
the tender surrealism of time poured from no radio
no photo no Armenia of moon or Luci (which means
moon in that quiet sky lowered into darkness and almond-
honeyed rose language no voice can match but thought
can burn or ignite alone or under the cool blue Colorado
sky dream gone going going) slow down and tell
stories in poetry of how her shyness fell when heated
with wine or kisses she'd allow herself to blossom somehow
to stretch out on that long gray-smoothing-plum sofa
in the livingroom of the sad red door precisely one block west
of his sweetly numbered Underwood days where he typed
all day and night the baddest stories and poems and letters
she'd stretch and spread and let her love come down like that
but never all the way just close enough to smile

THIRD STREET PROMENADE;
FULL MOON, SUNDAY NIGHT, SANTA MONICA

> *"The hands of the clock have stayed still*
> *at half past eleven for fifty years.*
> *It is always opening time in the Sailors Arms."*
> —Dylan Thomas,
> *Under Milk Wood*

The Buddhist approach to packing up after the gig
requires no time; it unfolds moment by moment—
a dirty shirt here, a lost button there, all the slips
of paper, cassettes and more cassettes, wet socks
wrung out and bagged in zipper-snagged plastic,
badly slowing slips of mind concentrated like sunlight.
Starlight is what we're made of, is how we function clearly.
There is no other way to get right down to the history
of getting out of town. Uncrowded increments of space
make possible the way time works, the way it plays.

The big, slick moon, the ocean, palms, the high-rise
film-set backdrop of this misty physical night, set in desert,
done up green and brown, and grandly watered—understood.
While joggers and power-walkers line and fill Ocean Avenue's
manicured edges, plentifully, clinically, oxygen must fend
for itself. Air, like love, lies largely where you find it.
Here in the sixth largest nation on earth, where dreaming
is an industry, where belief is everything, and sunshine God,
the century ends. Transition seems everything, content
gridlock; this life, this style of going away and coming back.

The drawbacks, come-ons, exquisite alibis and raps this road
life requires get matched and met by always coming home.
And where is home? The present moment, right now, wherever
travelers find themselves. Not only is home pre-sent; it's postpaid,
upgraded every moment, constructed of breathing-room and
nothingness: the perfect relaxation tool for any foolish voyageur.

Just as time unpacks itself and readies balanced, opened minds
—for sudden shifts in plans, a change of heart, dramatic drops,
earthquakes, the shutting down of freeways, re-routed baggage,
roots—so you book and pack again for the only place you know.

PRAGUE

Once the tough look of your strongholds soften,
the eye grows as tender towards you as the stark blue
leanness of skies fatty with cloud clusters. You, Prague,
helmeted and armored in your cold, hard, drop-dead history,
dreaming your relentless dream of becoming again and
again and yet again the most enticing of European cities.
In this New Europe you get to pick who goes fishing
for pleasures with you in your beloved green-black River Vlatava
that flows through you the way Smetana poured out
sound refinements of your big, fried deep-meat ways.
Like Mozart, like Franz Kafka, like all the hapless renters
who end up glorifying the very stops that gave them hell,
you pat your own back. In back and side streets packed
with crystal, good beer, Sex Boats, funny hats and wigs and
velvet everything the Slavic soul heels and toes.
Jesus, Hussites, the Medicis, the Gods of Tourism flourish.
The worlds you've toured, you bring them home to Prague.

EUROPEAN UNIONS

Would American pianist Henry Crowder
comment on this? Between two wars he played
Nancy Cunard, jazzed her press; The Hours swept
up into *Negro*, her devastating anthology.
Having cussed out her mother, inviting loss
(the Cunard Shipping Line), she gave up one real-life
fantasy, a vast wet dream of oceanic capitalism.
Early Mussolini had run them out of Italy,
where he'd been gigging yearly with homeboys,
Chicagoans; the times had no time for their likes.

Surreal, Paul Eluard had loved Cunard in a France
where Salvador Dali praised Hitler and thugs.
The notion that nations are best ruled by business,
had come back home to Britain and the rest of Europe.
Now that we live and breathe it hour by hour
(hostile takeovers, golden parachutes, stock options),
we still think of brown and black shirts, skinheads
when plain old-fashioned fascism comes up.
Prague's blues and nerve; a beautifully needed city
(Nazis needed it, now the EU); the blues and nerve
of being together, knowing the ropes, and bailing.

To have come all this way on blues and nerve
and no sleep says more than a lot for life.
Living—what is that? Were those people
at that mom & pop store Christina and I used
to shop at in Prague; that couple so proud
of their daughter's English in the winding
streetlight of summer, the broken cold
of winter bottles, paper bags, tomatoes, pears,
garlic, unbeatable Czech pilsner, eggplant,
like the summer of our parting, a fact?

SNOWY MORNING BLUES

in tribute to James F. Johnson
and Langston Hughes

New York, you know, has its New Yorks,
Manhattan her Queens, the Bronx
keepers of the flames with all their names intact.
Now that's a fact. Upside it, though,
you'll put your heart and everything
you know or thought you knew of snow.

When Snowy Morning Blues plays James P. Johnson's
game of catch-me-if-you-can, you can. He could, too.
New York ain't no last word, you know.
Nothing's what it used to be. And you, the you who sees
out past the end of the world, this snow, this wee wind-
fall he fells us with under eaves the way we all fall
under suspicion in detective movies. Blam!
Blame it on the blues, blame in on a blizzard.

Diamonded, grounded in its ice cream crisscross,
snow makes you take to the country again, harmonica in hand,
craving the guitar of a pianistic You-Gotta-Be-Modernistic
genius—you can't get into this. Let snow tell its own story.
Let the blues roll on. Let snow fall right on time this time
blue, blank, blackening the city-within-a-city christened
in Dutch: Harlem, Haarlem,
Haaaarrrrrlem.
Vermeer, beware.

OPENINGS

The door half-cracked, part-locked, a jar,
a pot to piss in, windows, sleeves,

escape by subway, jet, or car;
a tree lets go by shedding leaves.

You move from birth through death to life
and back again. Where do we go?

Where did we start? What drum, what fife
sounds our on-going ebb and flow?

THE HAWK TALKS

"Think clay, think pots, think wet-handed ways.
Think the world of anything or anyone you love
or can't or don't & think nothing of it.
Think ink if you re-write worlds; think pink
if you're a colorist; think singer if you're a song
& think beat if you're the drum." The hawk talks
to me at 56 differently than he did yesteryear.
He sends me dark, redeemable smiles that say:
"Steady yourselves, my friend. Think yourself
into the act, enough to act in your own behalf."

ONE WAY TO TAKE A HIT

The hardest hit to take aims for the heart.
In love, strung out, you swallow hard and duck.
Too late. No shots ring out, no poisoned dart
comes whizzing at you—zap! So what the fuck
connects? You're history, but something's odd.
The blindfold's gone, your hands aren't tied. There is
no disappearing license plate, no God
to greet, no hell. No Kosovo, no Paris.
The only sound: one heart still beating—yours.
If this were Sicily someone would scream,
or drag away the corpse, or order flowers.
Who put this contract out? What bleeding dream
dried up? What deal got spooked? The sorry room
love has to give itself. Who takes out whom?

SOLARIS

> *"Science—nonsense! We don't want to conquer space at all; we want to expand Earth endlessly. We don't want other worlds; we want a mirror."*
>
> —Dialogue spoken by Snouth
> in the Soviet film, *Solaris*
> (based on the novel by Stanislaw Lem)

Explore Earth infinitely, rock by rock, root by root,
inch by inch, hair by hair, pixel by pixel, tock by tock.
There was a way once to get back; not get even,
but to reach home without leaving the body.
Imagine the unsounded but fully heard voice
that clumps up within you, that fluffs into a hunch,
silver every time. If intimacy lit up like this,
all holiness could be speared and stuffed and mounted.
Thank God for invisibility, for the untraceable
trails we sink in, marking our journeys in electrical ink
upon mental score paper that reads us perfectly.
That thoughts are things is all the faith we need.
To think pure beauty, have it turn up in your arms
or at your feet or on your bourgeois walls means
business. To slow time down until the space between
moments stretches beyond the hours means eternity.
Unworldly gospel people who lean into the clouds
look for that uncloudy day. To others, matter matters,
nothing else, and business is business. Explore?

PRELUDE TO A KISS

in memory of Ella Fitzgerald

There was a time when singing or playing a ballad was almost the same as the whisper your lips make the instant before they pooch out and stretch, then reach to touch hers.

Her lips will feel the warm wind your whisper makes in the life-preserving urgency of moving mouth-to-mouth. Whole career moves, investments have been based on this, a kiss.

There at the after-whisper—when breath saith unto breath: "Death, go back out and wait in the car, baby, we got some unfinished business we need to take care of up in here"—there Ben Webster or Lester might pester you into listening to thrilling snapshots of their up-close worlds, where rivers and stars and cyclones and witch-hunts and hatred found and hounded them endlessly. But Ella's voice would graze the words and say: Psssst-psssst and Shhh-shhh.

Whenever Body Snatchers invaded, remember? Remember the Memorex commercial? Shattered, the glass itself was thinking: "Better this way than whoops! Better this than drunk-ass fans arguing. Who was best—Billie, Sarah, Dinah, Carmen or Ella?"

There she stood, or there she sat at piano, not playing, sometimes in pain—a twisted ankle, a mangled heart—wiggling around on that bench, whispering her bloodbeat to crowds in Spain, Brazil, Japan, the Netherlands, Australia, Oslo, L.A., Akron, Accra, Krakow, and O how they knew when her voice—a whip, a feather—was busy inventing universes they always thought had been in place all along.

Wrong. Ella Fitzgerald launched songs far more reliably than NASA launched spacecraft. She sent them spinning into orbits that ennobled, that ran rainbows around your shoulders.

We couldn't carry her around in that basket forever. Ella owned the world the way she earned our owning her. Every time her voice floats back, that kiss moves in, and then begins.

THE SOUND OF DREAMS REMEMBERED

> *"There is no ahead."*
>   —Rumi

In the soul-tunnel of my ear God hummed.
At the back of my dream Havana drummed
beneath and overall the moon-treed thoughts
that bloomed inside of me as ones and oughts
last night next door to this dream of the world,
listening to housemate Pam Houston's story unfurl
about the woman stalking her to France
and back to Utah, Provincetown. "The chance
of her turning up here in our mountain locale
is slim, isn't it?" I asked. Pam said, "Well, Al,
who knows? Nothing would surprise me, really."
That night—and maybe we were being silly—
Jay Gummerman and I locked the front door
to the ski house all we writers shared, more
to be safe than startled, in the big Squaw
Valley night, where starry sights unthaw,
where I could always count on what I dreamed
to mirror quiet heights; to lift what seemed
unreal and let it walk, talk, digitally,
the way the day curls with night to circle spiritually.

A SOLO FOR SULU

Here where night blows hot and cold with rain
at the end of October just starting, I signal you.

Not with smoke do my arms flail and my eyes
light up like the translated bodies of signers the deaf

deal with. To co-respond to you in poetry seams.
Dreams linger in language love never could do without.

PREZ IN PARIS, 1959

By 1959 he'd moved to Paris.
Prez wouldn't eat. Sweet alcohol harrassed
his system. Cooled, the jazz "To Be or Not
to Be"—withdrawn, a whisper—seemed a jot.

Once there'd been ways to get back at the world;
Ex-G.I. Prez had tried and tired. He hurled
himself now—hearsay, smoky horn—down-stage.
"Well, Lady Gay Paree, it's been a dog's age,"

he might've said. Or "Ivy Divey! Wrong!
The way that channel swims—too cold. This song
—the lyric's weak. We'll drown. No eyes, my man.
No, let's don't take it from no top. The band

can skip it." Prez. Monsieur le Président,
who played us what can work, and what just won't.

SISTER HOODZ

Some sisters do, too, truly love those jive artists, those
brothers they put down so stunningly in their stories,
their songs, their prayers; those pretty, irresistible
Mister Pitifuls, these Sexual Healers and Double
Dealers under the table, edge of the bed, hard-
grooving, smooth moving Mandingo Manchilds
with whom they'd sooner pull a nooner than a night.
From the top of their heads comes ho, comes
bitch, comes nothing so redeeming as a seven-year itch.

THE BLUES AD INFINITUM
(SAY AMEN)

The positively thrilling look of you
sometimes, like now, this very afternoon,
where Pittsburgh shimmers on the brink of fall,
where trees in clumps and copses (from the air)
look almost blue and swollen with the red
and gold of you; cerulean and ochre,
magenta, all those colors in between
the ones we grew and knew and drew before
Miss Raskin said, "Your basic yellows, greens
and reds and blues you've got to really learn.
Your browns and blacks and whites, your orange, your pink
all this is basic. You don't need the rest.
How many things around you look chartreuse?
Primary colors make up all the rest."

You heard her say that, didn't you? You were there;
invisible except for sneaky winks
you'd give me when I looked across the lake
for colors hip Miss Raskin wouldn't have known
if they'd sneaked up and bit her on the neck.

To school a bunch of hoodlums, what a gig
that must've been. New forms of lunacy
were getting off the ground around that time:
Dean Martin, Jerry Lewis, bebop jokes,
atomic bomb tests, witch hunts, Bird with Strings.

Attachments weren't our schtick; we aimed to please
ourselves, so when we drew, we'd draw her way
and then we'd switch; go back to what we liked.
Miss Raskin's color theories slid past us;
implosive, blue, they felt too close to home.
Whatever brown would warm, white might wash out;
whatever black denoted could blow up
right in our faces, detonate. The trick
(we learned it well) was just to chill.
Nobody said that then; we said, "Be cool."
But chill was what we meant, and what we did
until I learned from drawing that the page
exists as an extension of the world.

The world, as drawn by you, cartoons itself;
we color and re-color it the way
this town took back the red and iron rust
the hard Ohio River used to drag.
Once factory-smoked and steel-worked, Pittsburgh breathes.
Without you, without flame or thrill or light,
where would a lonesome traveler go to rest?
But time has never meant a thing to you,
or has it in some way helped you keep score?
You look so good, you make me feel all right.

THRIVING ON A RIFF

This feels like where it all pours in, this email,
male and female, these virtual squeezes under moons.
Its pleated, accordion playfulness connects
one set of sides with all the others. In rains whose color

changes every time we say hello, the bud idea goodbye
just will not grow. This feels like what the doctor meant
when she said, "Quiet country love, that's all you need."
I used to go to that doctor. A city girl from birth,

she grew like Perth. Don't play that song. Doctor's orders.
Saying it over and over, remembering; the whole,
big, quivering memory of why we're even here at all
comes clear. The stroke and key of it—a rose that rises.

THE OLD COUNTRY

In memory of Nat Adderley

All the old countries we freeze and thaw—
your Germany, my South, your Cuba, Vermont.
You talk about diminishing returns, the law
that governs Texas. What is it we want,
or need to haul or lug like Motorolas
of the blood? Beep! The mileage we squander
on these jumps from mayonnaise Minnesotas
to curry Calcuttas, from Tokyos you could wander
like spy-quality surveillance snapshots. Half
of you dwells in your dreaded origins. Beep!
Is this the constant wake-up call we laugh
about, then reconsider when we need to sleep?
Sometimes, in the middle of the night, drunk
on memory—the way your mother scrubbed a fish,
the way your father cried over the crusty trunk
jammed with photos all jumbled up, a swish
a gurgle; the pond and river-like wash of romance—
you freeze. You shiver through the old countries:
your Michigans, Ohios, Indianas, Lagos, France.
You draw lines, you push, the spongy boundaries
squeeze until they bleed. Beep! Old country fuzz;
its sad clarity; the sanctity of what is, what was.

FUZZY LOGIC

All milks, all clocks, all bets are off
when love wobbles into the picture.
Prose turns into poetry and, worse,
nobody knows the difference anymore.
Love buries itself, then erects its own
monuments: *Here Lies Chance,*
Your Last Perhaps to Bravely Breathe
Romance. Fuzzy logic rules the quick
and dead alike in this decomposing world
of wormy hard conceptions. Look yourself
right in the eye and see love live, love die.

CZECH FOOD LINGO
(JIDLO)

I take you in as sunlight, savor you
as air, as brath, as phtosynthesized
crust & flake or peel & seed:
the flavors of Prague waft by as smoke,
as sizzling oil, as onion plain enough,
as garlic freed from spells, as smells
the softness & sharpness of riverside eats.
Along the Vlatava, where bells toll dolefully
away from water, café dreams blossom
like the taste of peppers in your beery palate.
Potato & paprika cook long in the mind
before they fry up before us proof that sun,
light, fiery earth & water & air can be stored
& stared at with lip-smacking gusto.
The dogs of Prague speak Czech food lingo:
a drowsy line of patter—Prague's platters.

CONNECTED AT 44666 BPS

Getting up off the potty of email
and back onto the runway of real life,
you find yourself amazed that rain
still falls to wet the world with what
we need and crave and steal yet cannot call.
Such digital distraction sings its praise
songs to willing global villagers alone.

Alone, the information lake tides
hide in surf sand down your eardrums,
send subtle solos jazzing through your veins.
Does blood know its buzz logs in at 98.6?
Does light at night reflect upon the speed
it needs to sharply tune the contours of a dream?
"I sting, therefore I bee," Sam Pickering says.

To places where all subtle forces hang
is where we're headed on this dancing beam
of logarithms, codes and ciphered fuzz.
To look straight at your lover, to feel her
breathing in real-time, exhaling all the time
there ever was or ever needs to be—hits close.
Now you can email heaven that you're home.

ON THE ROAD WITH BILLIE

Your heart might have been beating like a hammer,
but this was not a drama I needed, much less staged.
Black and Catholic out of Baltimore. What else?
Who did you think you were? I thought I knew.
The sound of dreams remembered—that's who.
You covered the waterfront. We dogged the road.

There was no way those clouds were going anywhere
without us drifting right along. "No quarrels,
no insults, and all morals"? Hardly. In flooded Oregon
we had to get used to wet and wet and wet, get
their jokes about web feet, and get it that patches
of blue that popped up oddly around 4 p.m.,

wake-up time, just outside Portland. God bless
the child who knew you didn't need to drown
your past regrets in coffee and cigarettes, when
we soaked up hours so ripe with rain we learned
every *DETOUR AHEAD* sign by heart. Sex didn't fix.
In this itinerary, the lovesick sound of you worked

more than willows. That trip you took on the train
to get there, remember? "When it rains in here,"
you sang, "it's storming on the sea." Baby, speak
for yourself. You were the one as hard to land
as the Isle de France. Taking a chance on love,
you took a fall. You had your songs to keep you warm.

You wished on the moon. "Some other spring," you
sighed, then slipped through June, a sieve, and got
so high you couldn't get back by the Fourth of July.
The local fuzz, a fan, knowing I'd be freaked,
rang up all sing-song, mocking you, and said:
"That love won't turn the trick to end despair."

Billie, the tricks you turned, the twists blues took.
Why people tear the seams of other folks' dreams
was all it ever was about for you. Am I unfair?
Some kiss did cloud my memory. Still, I smuggled
you to Seattle. At every stop that we made,
I thought about you, too. The crack of dawn

and that crack you peeped through, the one leading
back—was all the crack there was back then.
When the war broke out and opium split town,

up jumped smack, and you and all your hophead
pals went down and copped. "You go to my head,"
you groaned. Where did it all go? Where did you go?

"I get no kick from cocaine"? "Mere alcohol
doesn't thrill me at all"? It made you smile awhile.
The war? They changed the chords, the beat,
you know, it never stopped. They changed the bill.
The War on Poverty, it bombed, but War on Drugs,
it's on a roll, like we were on a roll—April in Paris,

Autumn in New York, Nice Work If You Can Get It;
as if you'd be waiting for me always in the doorways of
Trailways and Greyhounds and train depots, small
hotels with wishing wells, and all the grand hotels;
the same old fine brown frame, sweating like an orchid,
and your heart beat so that you could hardly speak.

OCTOBER OBBLIGATO

The rain of it, the housing sun, the paint,
the painters loud and Mexican, "Ay, ay!"—
just write it like it is. Be cute, be quaint
if that helps get you started. Do the sky,
do clouds, do wind. Do faith, the way leaves grow
out green, then yellow, redden, age and fall.
You love October. Why? Because you know
this cycle spins its wheels until you call
it quits. What do houses made of rain or sun
or dawn or unnamed colors owe this world?
Zip. Nada. Not a thing. Their deal was done
before the deed, a trick, and rent, its showgirl,
got one big leg up on October. Wet,
the autumn home you love is what you get.

DEPRESSION, BLUES, FLAMENCO, WINE, DESPAIR

Depression, blues, flamenco, wine, despair—
sunk in, they make you cross your heart and die
for hope. Dark times come at you; they don't care.
"So deal with this," they say. And so you buy
the pain and stress, the restlessness—the works:
low back pain, aches and limps, the twitch
of fear your face betrays.

                John "Dizzy" Birks
Gillespie's cheeks puffed out (fat love an itch
scratched by the trumpet at his goateed lip),
they said: "Take chances, stretch, jump at the sun.
You just can't spend your whole life acting hip.
Be corny sometimes. Have yourself some fun.
You can't be cool forever, so relax."

Diz knew puffed cheeks were anything but chic,
but when you closed your eyes you heard him axe
infinitives, split atoms, hairs. You speak
that tongue—curves, flatlands, all of it. You do.

You understand the hoodoo stab of hurt;
the blues, their messy messages, a few
trashed hopes, some lame goodbyes, her skirt,
your coat, the folded jeans, wet tights. Black night
is falling all around you in the rain.
Dark times, dark times can fix you in the light
of reason, recognition, lasers, pain.

A POEM FOR LATE-BLOOMING EARLY RISERS

for jackie

Late at night, or early morning never is the point;
each is a field we reach and wander, separate or whole.
The thrill of being present in this dream we walk awake
may never die. Who wants it to? Not I, not you,

party to this slow, unfolding story we take turns telling
in keyed eighth notes, quarter notes, half notes; in holes
between connections, too, and in thoughts we do not have
to send or have come in. Telegraphy, telepathy—

what do they share uncommonly? Late-blooming early
risers need not respond. May all your sleepy wakefulness
and mine tug us snugly home inside ourselves each night
when moons go slack, space out, or pale. Night speaks,

and morning answers afternoon. Day by day the hours sing
their hushes and hurrahs to one another along a chain
of sounded light so brilliant that sometimes we each can feel
and count the beats a heart makes when its loving turn comes up.

BREAK A LEG, GET A HAND

Most of the cast got nervous before the gig,
Jenny got crazy afterwards. Whole rest-
of-the-nights she would spend bent over herself,
egging on an ego that might've been better off
laying eggs than listening for cues or prompts.
She couldn't figure it out, but it usually took
the same form. Audiences would rise to their feet
and clap themselves raw after she hit that last note,
a perfect high C over C, as clear as the bell-like
tone of Armstrong or Yma Sumac in their prime,
or the classic Cleo Laine in Jenny's own time.
She never failed to wangle the finale away from
everyone else night matinee, early or late; fate
didn't have a thing to do with it, Chicago, Boston, New
Haven, New York, Toronto, St. Paul, Seattle, L.A.,
Dallas, New Orleans, Atlanta, she was stealing
more than the show, she was stealing apple orchards
and whole orange groves, and yet—diamonds to ashes,
gold to dust—she would dash every bit of trust
you would think our backstage applause and the crowd's
signalled. It wasn't until Jenny decided to think
about giving it up that she started seeing a shrink.
He was crazier than she was, that man, he said,
"What will you do when you get to the point where
you can't perform or go out on stage anymore?"
Then you'll have to stay at home and bore your family,
your friends and anybody who'll listen with stories
that only focus on your failures, and none of the glories
of being the center of attention from 15 to 50."
And Jenny said, "What! And get out of show business?"

WATER, FIRE, AIR, THE EARTH, THE WIND

In drizzly, gloomy, womb wet modes of light
rebirth begins. Its mood of candle-power, and her burn-
down melts whatever flamed before with peeling grace.
Like rain pop-speckling the roof at night, a garden wall
of frogs and well-flagged seeds, the days, twice lit,
begin their trip inside this moment—dawn.
No cyber-trail of fire works this show.

Tough skateboard kids in gritty Edgware Road
make their leaps in light as agilely as any banker might,
as mathematicians Alan Turing or Stephen Hawking might.
The differences they split now is how they'll weather-
watch and work their roomy territories.

Where financiers and brokerage cheats predictably hedge
their greedy bets against alerts, and where poets
of the infinitely uncrunchable cosmologize,
these wise kids see, and, seeing, jump. The only sun
they know lies under wraps of cloud, prediction, interest shifts
all odds. Unbeatable, candle warmth reconstructs
the room that water falls around, where all things new
start out; still safe, still buried, wet, adrift, aflame.

> *Westminster*
> *London 1999*

GIVING THE DRUMMER SOME

L.H.O.O.Q.
(pronounced: *Elle a chaude au cul*)
—Early 20th century "ready-made"
by Marcel Duchamp

She's all fucked up and French, he knows.
He knows the cultural pressure she's under,
knows what she's started, knows what won't end.
The big sky color of her eyes, the European
complication she's hooked into, all that shit,
he knows it well. At first he didn't know much French,
but he got it together pretty quick. He got the rhythm
of it, its round and nasal loveliness, the underflow,
the way sometimes she sounded like a horn; other
times like reeds. There'd been a point he'd read about
when the Mediterranean had been like a Muslim lake;
the Moors had come that close to taking France.
Now here they were again. Back. And standing
unbathed, backless, blue, bikini'd, blunt—her butt:
two round vowels not yet moist with towels because
she liked the sound of funky in her proud tongue—
fon-quiii as you wanna be, gallant Gallic mama!
How long could he hang in Paris between gigs
How thick did he wish to get with Klook
and Griff and Kenny and Dexter and Mal
and, before them, Don Byas, Sidney Bechet?
Steve Lacy had hipped him when he'd first hit town:
"Dance, man. Do your dance and keep moving."
For a class drummer, he figured, I ain't doing bad.
It wasn't the French invented surrealism; it was Americans.
Jazz, too. It was time to drag Monique, he decided,
over to the stereophonique to debut his new CD.
As Romeo once said to Juilet, "Haven't we met?"
He had no doubt that he could straighten her out.

IN THE SIERRAS

for Oakley & Barbara Hall

Way up here, where sky comes close
to calling all the shots, where
photographers, geographers and gopher-
loathing golfers and creature-comfort joggers,
where bikers, hikers, wrecking crews and
hoarse writers alike mount slow invasions;
here, where whole fields, whole hills heal
and mountains make big money mean,
peace speaks its native tongue.

Way up here, where sky comes close,
where stakes grow vast, where the last
and first run neck and neck, where loveliness
lays herself on every line at once;
up here, where far and close dissolve,
where the Sierras do not err and terror
cheapens. Sleeplessness like formlessness
must nest at midnight-lighted height.
Peace gets and takes its chances.

TOUCHED DOWN

From skin-locked silence, the buzz begins.
On ears that know big differences it falls;
love fails to know the power of nothing said.

The sweetest zones get covered inch by inch.
A star gets born and born again inside your ear.
Sweat sticks the buzz to muscle and to breath.

YO-YO MA, WHAT HE JUST PLAYED

"Libertango" from Soul of the Tango:
The Music of Astor Piazzolla

Was it an aeon, was it even a year, or even an ago?
There was a sandy hill, plants all around its edges,
the sway of a sea that probably saw the sadness
of them being happy, they thought, under no moon,
barely a sun – thin as whispers. And there
on a slowly sinking hill she placed her hand in his
and he smoothed his over hers and a yelp,
many yelps spilled over the rim of their dune,
screeching at the slow joy of the Pacific. Oh, God,
why must we feel time as force, as feasibility,
when one unstolen moment would do us?

I CAN'T GET STARTED

after Vernon Duke & Ira Gershwin

Isn't this the way it always ends up?
The deepest of nights, the ripest of moons,
the fragrance of magnolia and gardenia—
dueling sorceresses. And you are all I want.
The August air wafts the whole world
to where you, in your bikini and gown, rest
beside me in tropical summer whites.
Without making eye contact, we can feel
the voltage. The same alternating current
that makes our thoughts tremble and wobble
in their synaptic tracks stops us cold.
Speechless just will not describe what I seem
to be becoming, nor does breathless cut much ice.
Spellbound? Spellbound does come close.
This has got to be the night, I thought.

Sweet Barbados it is not. There is no more
revolution in Spain for me to settle
(although I have fixed elections in Florida).
OK, beauty, there is no denying this
must be some kind of powerful feeling
we're playing with here all by ourselves.
Circling the globe and charting the North Pole,
hobnobbing with presidents and bitch
superstars, starring in pictures and specials
myself, going one on one with Tiger Woods
and each of the Williams Sisters—kid stuff.
In my bourgeois house, by my brand new pool,
my late-life Ph.D thesis about to be a book,
my savvy stock portfolio healthy and trim
like this new body to which you get
my initial public offering, and Oprah
just left me some choice voicemail.
Tell me, sweet thing, please—how come
I find myself blessed with everything
this system provides, and still I can't get you?

CONJUGAL VISITS

Christ, Jahveh, Buddha, and your master, though
At bitter enmity, make peace on this:
Where love is, there the living instant is
And death is not, nor mourning, but the flow
Of timesless giving. Look, I sought a tomb,
And generous sleep has given me a glowing womb.

—Gladys Schmitt
(#23: Sonnets for An Analyst)

CONJUGAL VISITS

By noon we'll be deep into it—
   up reading out loud in bed.
Or in between our making love
   I'll paint my toenails red.

Reece say he got to change his name
   from Maurice to Malik.
He think I need to change mine too.
   Conversion, so to speak.

"I ain't no Muslim yet," I say.
   "Besides, I like my name.
Kamisha still sounds good to me.
   I'll let you play that game."

"I'd rather play with you," he say,
   "than trip back to the Sixties."
"The Sixties, eh?" I'm on his case.
   "Then I won't do my striptease."

This brother look at me and laugh;
   he know I love him bad
and, worse, he know exactly how
   much loving I ain't had.

He grab me by my puffed up waist
   and pull me to him close.
He say, "I want you in my face.
   Or on my face, Miss Toes."

What can I say? I'd lie for Reece,
   but I'm not quitting school.
Four mouths to feed, not counting mine.
   Let Urban Studies rule!

I met him in the want ads,
  we fell in love by mail.
I say, when people bring this up,
  "Wasn't no one up for sale."

All these Black men crammed up in jail,
  all this I.Q. on ice,
while governments, bank presidents,
  the Mafia don't think twice.

They fly in dope and make real sure
  they hands stay nice and clean.
The chump-change Reece made on the street
  —what's that supposed to mean?

"For what it costs the State to keep
  you locked down, clothed and fed,
you could be learning Harvard stuff,
  and brilliant skills," I said.

Reece say, "Just kiss me one more time,
  then let's get down, make love.
Then let's devour that special meal
  I wish they'd serve more of."

They say the third time out's a charm;
  I kinda think they're right.
My first, he was the Ace of Swords,
  which didn't make him no knight.

He gave me Zeus and Brittany;
  my second left me twins.
This third one ain't about no luck;
  we're honeymooners. Friends.

I go see Maurice once a month
  while Moms looks after things.
We be so glad to touch again,
  I dance, he grins, he sings.

When I get back home to my kids,
    schoolwork, The Copy Shop,
ain't no way Reece can mess with me.
    They got his ass locked up.

HOW THE FLOWER FLOURISHES

Unnumbered & floating
technician-free

smooth
a spore unfolding fast

upon pond-like lake surfaces
spread across unlogged zones of time

this colored burst of meaning
leans peeping from her axis

in lighted directions
every first & last one of them
heated

all 360 degrees precisely memorized
enough to become spontaneous

enough to allow the marvelous
to mimick or memorize herself

FURTHER ADVENTURES OF THE DOLLAR

The Dollar said, "This hustling and scuffling
gets on my nerves. Besides, I haven't even
been at this stuff anywhere near as long
as the Deutschmark or the Pound. The Franc
gets on my nerves the way it hangs out with the Yen,
and lately ain't nothing I do can turn heads,
much less tides." The Dollar liked the Swiss Franc,
though, he liked her solid ground. But the Pound
it was that took him out of commission, so that
from the start the Dollar knew the score.

Dollar said, "Yeah, this shit gets old real fast. I never
intended to last anyway; I only wanted to prevail.
If a Dollar could go to jail, that's where I'd be—
locked down where people would be forced to find
another way to be current, to do their hard hellos,
their soft good-buys." And so the Dollar disappeared
just long enough to fall in love. You're wondering,
aren't you? Where in the world would a dollar find
a girl, a lover anyway, to do his loose
and crazy thing with? Well, there were two:
Miss Swiss and a lovely young Yen he'd always had
his eye on in peril and through thick. The dick
of dollardom grew hard, grew firm.

And walloping the competition, Mr. Dollar
was heard to holler: "OK, so now that push has come to shove,
excuse me while I slide into one of those
free falls,
since
nothing
can
stop
me
now.

Just let me float."

HOURS BEFORE TOUCHDOWN IN LONDON

for Christina

She's sleeping now, or is she wide awake?
The thought of her reaches my fingertips;
the swelling sway of dreams. Soft rock, a lake.
A skimmer's touch, the quake of tides, sea-whips
we'll swing and crack—thought-bubbles always pop.
She'll greet me with firm, proper English tact,
but once the coast is clear her guard will drop.
Her elegance will warm. She'll squeal. In fact,
to look for signs of love when I arrive,
to wish or long for anything misleads.
When up against itself the mind will jive,
cajole and make you think it meets your needs.

The plane will land, she'll meet me at my gate;
all hot-shoed, flushed, and dressed to understate.

DEXTER

for Dick & Sarah Maxwell

In slow-blowing zones
the dream floats on
tough
unbitten
nail-hard swiftness

Catnapped
the beat expands
to match a scratchy brush stroke

Drummers
beware

(MY BABY LOVE)
THE WESTERN MOVIES

The funk-encrusted ghosts of Calamity Jane,
Wild Bill Hickock and New York City-born Billy
the Kid have reared up and crisscrossed the continent
in fluttering wisps of nerve.

                    Pictures we get
from their hoofbeat soundtracks prove that fiction
can run, it can outlast fashion. The sheer despair
of all those dead heroes could be riding
on subway trains of glory, trains of thought;
not all of it got washed up in legend.

Don't go falling in love with legends. Myths, OK,
but legends—be careful. *The Great Train Robbery,*
Buck and the Preacher, Butch and Sundance,
reigns of terror, a reigned-in quick-draw artist,
and a heavy rain of credits
have more in common than we once believed.

A TOAST TO CHARLES BUKOWSKI

Clipboard elegance ain't got nothing on you
back fresh from bar room fronts & fights &
the fakery of youth more invented than avoided.
In dauntless nights Longfellow's Evangeline
   could've even cut,
you would've been Gabriel, her unkeepable old man.

No wasteland-blasting trumpeter, either,
but a true accordionist. Kicked out of Acadia,
you'd be just the angry immigrant (a German-
born Pole) to squeeze or be squeezed.
Up yours, up yours, up yours, King George!

We're talking literature here, Prince Charles;
talking walking to New Orleans in your winter
   underwear.
Troilus & Cressida, Orpheus & Eurydice, Ulysses
   & Calypso.
Bukowski & Linda? Nah, Bukowski & Nemesis
(*Si Semen* might be the early to middle bop take).
How's that for running what was underground
   back into the ground?

But, really, Buk, I got news for you: All those French,
those Dutch, those German, those break-away
   Muscovite & Tokyo kids
who hit DeLongpre Avenue to re-be Bukowski, to re-play
   your L.A., alcohol & all,
they now re-claim those colorful alley & gutteresque
frontiers you & Tom Waits so handsomely zapped.

NEW AGE ESPIONAGE

*On learning about the all-out police
surveillance program (directed at black
communities in particular) in
Newcastle.*

The Great Britain of saying goodbye occurs
in burrs of now, right here where thought-
flow chokes sleeplessness and silent light listens.

Rain listens closely in this glistening light
that makes soil jovial, alluvial, alive—
even in London. Evening or morning, high noon

or midnight, lovers, who leave little or nothing
to chance, who hardly take heart in parting,
can taste time, can taste light, can taste

the outlets to so many seas, but sweetness, no.
And here's the joke: The torture of departure
churns in them, undoes their blues, their sunken pasts,

their future trysts. In this unquiet canvas
of stormcloud sky (the other end of painter Mark Toby's
Seattle embattlements) hellos fade out of focus,

out of date. But out of sight will not mean out of mind.
How simple it had seemed: the sailing out, the swimming back;
the push and pull of love pinpointed yet displaced.

Attention, Video Surveillance, Spies at Newcastle:
the coal you carry may very well become the coal you burn.
The rain of going away and coming back drives out drought.

The only time there'll ever be is now.

ONE HUNDRED-YEAR-OLD JAZZ HEAD TELLS ALL

1/

Locus. Focus. Johnny Hodges, his chest
swollen with rhapsodic pride, explains
why he got it bad and that ain't good.
The energy he's putting out and giving up
might not take up 15, 16, 18 long-distance
phonecalls in the midwestern midnight or,
in another vein, from four down to five a.m.
But Rabbit is still alive and all in place.
Locus. Focus.

2/

            We shifting now from the world
of jazz reportage, the tabloidal blahs. We
into the throbbing, swollen truth of it, Rufus.
Gradations, that's what we plunging into.
Plumbing might sound more like it; the ways
trombone players will wah-wah and growl at you
all off-key and on, talking like Rabbit can sing.
We music-makers, we time zappers. We got it
down yet and still we all the time going for it
the way that poet Simon Ortiz always be
going for the rain. We got it, all right, but
got it and getting it—good, bad, moody,
muddied—was that ever the point?

3/

                        The real
"Rabbit" Hodges, the brutal Ben Webster of it,
simmers down to this: It's kissers, not kisses,
that sometime cause the blues. Just like hugs
can cause your chest to swell. And if, just *if,*
you in your solar night or lunar afternoon

have trouble with this, all you got to do is stand,
sit, lie, or squat. Focus. Be still and know.
Then allow these master explainers to detain you
with as heavy a hit of infinity as you can take.
Locus, I call it. Kissers just can't go it alone.

THE TORTURE OF DEPARTURE

for Christina

Not even in my blackest dress,
my warmest tears, our bedside candle
blown out again or lit, could you guess
the rest of this mess. Steaming, tranquil,
it goes like this: We think we lose
by leaving, letting go. Leftovers heated,
then warmed up yet again can taste like blues;
some sweaty, worried line. Repeat as needed.

Released, these leaving blues sweet-talk
me into buying my own uneven stories.
You know the score. I'm free to walk
away unscathed; no fear, no worries,
no telling me this and telling me that,
no sudden change of key, no new menu.

And when the time arrives to flat
out fly away, whatever I intend you
simply say. You say, "Baby, this is the heart
of what it means to miss; this is
the torture of departure; the scary part
where airport hugs; precise, remembered kisses,
courage and touch and luck and such collide."

All-evening voyages through parks
and borrowed blocks, the summer ride
the city takes night for; remarks
gone unheard by the ear, but caught.
Put on my blackest formal gown
and cry. Let wet light turn the thought
of goodbye, gone, all upside-down.

To turn it all around (or inside-out)
shows what this blameless blueness is about.

SKIN TIGHT

*for Helen Bigelow
& Lorraine Cappareli*

Holding it all together, through feasts and fasts;

sealed or see-thru, permeable or waterproof;

stretched around this squirming world, where nothing lasts

except exquisite quicksand squiggles; the true roof

of the world, inseparable from what it houses

and, with blood-tied closeness, contains, protects—

pure spirit, at one with whatever it espouses.

We live in this. It does not live in us. Complex?

COLD SNAP

Science, a way of knowing, sees through fronts.
Science, a way of knowing, sees above all
the raw, erasable beauty of equations,
the mathematical eloquence of a freeze.

Where Vincent Van Gogh and Charlie Parker met
outside of time, their space remains
as charged and changed with color as it was with doves,
and that's the rub. Fahrenheit or Celsius,
warmth seems our hero but only when we consider
the great sea-change that occurs
above absolute zero. Does the float and cost
of air along flight lanes above the tropics hurt?

Hunkered down in Reykjavik, two women
consider the cost of a budget vacation in Bangladesh.
It becomes possible to go away, to withdraw
without leaving your mind in this world
of departures and arrivals, and on a schedule
that makes fun of owls and the quickening
of weather patterns sensitive to chips, to charters,
  to travelers checks.

TANGO

You're going to dance with the tiger.
Don't worry, your life is in danger.
Remember your instructions. Listen up.
And suffer, motherfucker, this is the tango."
　　　—Enrique Fernández
　　　(from the jacket notes
　　　for Astor Piazzolla's
　　　Zero Hour)

A tango of Mickey Mouses and Argentine wine?
That was their ticket, feckless as flypaper.
Slum lord night, what traps did you drum up for them
in those rose-strewn suburbs where freeways hum
on either side of their slumber, where medicated
mornings spin out of control and tulips turn
into crickets that dance, igniting the negotiable light
of afternoons? Paris could never jolt them now,
nor Buenos Aires or any of those pretty cities
where the tango made its name, where finally
it turned respectable like its off-color cousins —
the waltz, the blues.

　　　　　　Loose-hipped, broken-legged,
its accents fleshed out in the wrong places
(in squalid, unwashed bourgeois minds, in lies),
the tango safeguarded many a dangerous evening.
Vehement entertainment, maybe; ballroom rapture, yes.
The tango met them head on, hard, making and gaining
its points, propositioning its sway step by step
at off-hour stops the heart will always make.

FIVE

in memory of pianist Bill Evans
(1929–1980)

1/

In quiet, well-grazed groves,
up trees no player need reach,
some young squirrels,
scampering on breadfruit alone,
feel and even know they are forsaken
the way it ought to be for feeders.

2/

Out in the low fields at night
no one knew which way to turn
for canteloupe—
but watermelon, hey, don't you know?
All those seeds, all that red,
all that sugar going, "Juice, Juice, Juice!"
Oooo, the wet ripe rhapsody of fruit.

3/

Did somebody's child just rediscover moonlight?
Where would any of us be without that stuff?
What player hasn't hit that lick
a hundred times at least? What light
hasn't shone through keyboards under glass,
the sea an octave away? Smother me
under your pillowing spell.
Roll me in the dirty boogie-woogie of your light.

4/

O go for it! You can't fake these ultra-rhythms,
or can you? The way, the road, the distance
to Bali is the same as to Cairo. Karo Syrup
yourself all over like June. Bust out, break
free. Can the beat be everything? Maybe not,
but this is where we either jump back or
kick down the gate. Fax that back to Heaven.

5/

Hello, rain, so it's you again,
this time deluging Duluth. So where
do we go from here? What kind of thunder
are you putting us under this time?
Maple leaf don't stand a chance. And, birch,
forget it. There is in your attitude
and lean a summer just begun yet all but gone.
In telling squalls you make your soft, moist points.
Squashed by stars and hills and green air,
paned and spaced or squeezed between clouds,
we're moving now; call off your waltz.
Count off your classy blues and count us in.
The station's sounding smaller as we go.
The clouds we've shaped. The smile, the wave
the lake makes feels hipper too. Some gig!
Sweet sleep, slide slowly, gently, cleanly
through this bubbling blood of ours.

UP VERNON'S ALLEY

for the great bassist
Vernon Alley

His smile can light up wood as good as pluck.

All spark, no match, his finger's on some fuse

hooked up to soul; an ammunition truck.

Whole worlds go up when Vernon plays the blues.

THE LIVING TV ACTRESS CHANNELS
AN ANCIENT PLAYWRIGHT
(Or, WHAT THE STAGE WHISPERS)

Stage settings all, these star-clogged
play by plays—the lines you blow, the scenes
  you steal!

How do you build a plot not based on love?
What venue doesn't truly lie in you?
What can't you air that others won't tune in?
Without the scene and all its catches,
without the scene imagined and played out,
  you collapse.

And in your sad descent, collected and reflective
while you fall, mute language fails again.
Words worn down to their soles can't walk you there,
though where you have to go is closeby, quiet,
  and for real.

THE SLAVE SHIP DESIRE

> *"As for the New England slave trade—which, along*
> *with rum and opium, turned the kind of get-rich-quick*
> *profits in its day that international drug trafficking does*
> *now—that industry would not be launched until 1638,*
> *when the first Africans arrived in Boston on the slave*
> *ship Desire."*
> —Al Young
> *African American Literature:*
> *A Brief Introduction and Anthology*

Human cargo's what we're talking here;
a boat piled high, groaning, in fact, beneath
the strain of expectation factored in.
On board stuff hogged up space, turned soon-to-be.
Straight ahead and bright, the salt-sweet taste
of sweat and sacrifice, you couldn't spit it out.

Like opium, gold and rum, like land enough
to grow bigger eyes than food gone belly up,
the money's there. Like sugar or tobacco,
crack cash crops then as now, like coal,
September wheat, October cocoa, like unslit
porkbellies, like Jesus crossed with sex and
shoot-em-ups, like Anglo Franco Banco American futures.

Desire the boat; the streetcar's still to come.
Where human beings want, crossroads get jammed,
get all tied up. Whoever blocks escape routes
gets locked in, too. NO EXIT signs shine just fine
in the dark, and anger glows. Picture a boat
that crowds you, over-sized; a load of woe
there is no way around—a slave ship named Desire.

TALK-BACK RADIO GETS BACK

After Rodney King, even the new police chief
insisted that the "n" word no longer mattered,
did not count. "After all, when Cincinnati
Reds owner Marge Shott called two of her hottest
properties 'million-dollar niggers,' you can't deny
the compliment she was paying them. Marge was just
putting her money where her mouth was, calling
a spade a spade, dig?"

                        While angry waves washed over
and out beyond L.A., splashy, walkie-talkie, wild-eyed,
such underdog states as Oklahoma, Michigan, Montana and Idaho
got hurt and hard hit first. Next came Alabama
which had barely in the nick of time revived its venerable
Chain Gang. Stripes went pretty with more than flags.
Next stop: Corporal Punishment. Or, as one old colonel
put it: "Gentlemen, let's stick the cane back in sugarcane."

Meanwhile back on the Internet, where webmasters
had work cut out for them, unreconstructed patriots—
of sound constitution and wired—slipped
out of their pyres and crypts. Even AOL, Well widows
and get-a-life nerds heard the warnings, saw the bugles.
Posses lit out hot on the tracks of freedom-
hungry fugitives on the Information Highway.

All evidence, it seemed, and not just some,
kept leading and pointing back to headquarters.
Stymied, forced to mask and shred, both pigmy police
and Big Pig alike purged and erased their departments
clean to the vanishing point, where air already thin
grew raggedier, threadbare. Quickly all evidence
of the living truth, all signs of life began to disappear.
As for crimes not committed by Middle East terrorists,
authorities dealt with them off-handedly, off-color, off-screen.

EASY OVERHEAD

Can working the hot look of lovers and dreams
into what cool clouds might be thinking
of a glittering moment, or a lifetime of wanting
to be happy at the next exit ever easily end?

Imagine the histories of all clouds
in embryo, risen like music
from watery earth spirits heated,
sparked by fire, blown by wind.
Where do they come from,
where do they go?

People say if you've seen one cloud
you know them all. How can that be?
Just smell for yourself these perfumed clouds
hovering at the shadowy end of day
over a floating Paris, a saddening Paris;
a Paris even Helen of Troy would have to call dull.

How delicious the gypsy-like trickle
of Frenchified rain;
South-silenced rain that wets my glistening head;
a food of clouds digesting in my ears.

ELEVATOR OVER THE HILL

after Carla Bley

That was one evil elevator,
had a mind of its own.
It took you where it wanted
and brought you back
when it felt like it.

This elevator went in for trying
to crush people in its doors,
and woe unto the unwary passenger
who stuck an arm out to stop it.

This elevator would just as soon snap
a limb just like—like you would
a popsicle stick. If you pressed 10,
it stopped at 2, 3, 6 and
stuck at 7. Of if for some reason
it whisked you all the way
to the floor of your desire,
the door wouldn't open. You could ring
the alarm but no one would ever be there to help.

This elevator reeked continuously
of strong disinfectant, unpleasant perfumes
and colognes, take-away fast food, garbage
and farts, illicit cigars and even reefer some nights.
Sometimes you suspected it of substance abuse.

This elevator was a bring-down; it had a strong will.
It must've been, it had to be over the hill.

A LIZARD CONSIDERS THE SEASON

Upward floating
without
sky 1, sky 2, sky 3,
the open-domed light
of blue & low overhead,
this stillness the color
of late September.

Sadness plays
no place in
such spacious unraveling
of skin dried out as breeze,
as heat.
Hot, surf faces south.

Easy, rock, now,
easy, tree.
Touch me, smooth me,
wrinkle me here,
rough me up there.
Reach me where no blue blaze has
sunned or burned before.

Do I blacken
like old silver, neglected?
Do I shine in my climb the way joy resides
not around the corner but just beneath
the surface of these angles inched in &
out of dartable morsels & dots
that feed the lion of light?

Cool light,
fathom me, please,
& fatten all paths that lead away
from crows
on frosty eaves.

Alone in my aloneness,
I ooze
blue night.

BIG BOPPER FOR BEGINNERS

It took post-grad on top of post-
grad course, but finally he began
to understand what we talk about when
we talk about love—talk about, tell about,

cry about, sing about love, ooo, baby,
that's what I like. The freshman knew only
how to outwit the lonely part of himself
weaned on cinematic champagne and flowering

hearts on grand, green sleeves. Chantilly lace
and a pretty face. He dwelled in outer space.
Unconscious is far too kind a word; the fool
was dumb. Today you'd put it another way.

Now they'd say: The dumbing-down of love
would've rolled right off of him like a long-legged goose
like a rubber off his dick, like a duck.
He saw beauty, histories of mystery, eyes

that flirt, the heart that hurts, hot hair,
a ponytail dangling down. His angle, moreover,
was to clown in the back row during lecture,
relishing impressions he longed to lay down

hard on one big-eyed girl he would build
his world around for ages to come. Dumb?
The boy was tetched. Too lazy for sections,
he sketched and dreamed he would ease through blue-

books and quizzes by the skin of his curve.
He lasted this way for years on nerve and juice.
But when it came time to hang and act loose,
to make a run for the border, to take the New Order

("I want the house, I want my health care back,
and I'm the one who really needs the Nordic Trac"),
he realized what he had; his degree was undergrad.
It took post-grad course on top of post-

grad course, but spinally, finally he began
to get it, to understand what we talk about when
we talk about, hawk about, take tests, invest in
and get psyched about, and what we still like about love.

BATH

This entry into water seems enough
sometimes, the only way the body can
let mind be on its way; float loose like steam.
Wherever reckless thinking shoves, mind trips
and falls. This ball and chain of thought will weigh
us down, will hold us hostage at gunpoint
until hot water softens our hard heads;
until the secret self takes charge and says:
"Hey, this whole deal is backwards, don't you think?
Aren't I supposed to tell you what to do
instead of being dragged around by you?"
A bath can force the issue, clear the way
for arms and legs and hands and necks and backs
to loosen up their holds, let tensions go
the way of bubbles down the drain. Fuck stress.
Immersion in a warming, soapy tub
or in some backwoods river full of sun
is all the body needs to feel itself
forget itself again. Evaporate.

THE COMEBACK

Some stuff in composites
and nano manufacturing might
make love cheaper than a steel car

body with capital costs just a tenth
as big. Mister Bigshot will know
who he is by then, when energy

gets whittled down to the Duncan
and the Creeley and the Scalapino
of save. Radical simplification

—that's what we're sipping
and guzzling here. The toast
I propose (instead of using electricity

to break down sunlight I use hydrogen)
goes like this: Here's to humpbacks
and backpacks and razorbacks and scissor-

backs and paperback hacks and sacks.
Forget the facts. Under new language legi-
slation proposed by GOP (Giddy Old Poetry)

leaders, sentiment, like peppermints
and parliaments, betrays a far more ancient
origin than stars and alchemists.

And sentiment (a kind of condiment
to winners; liniment to losers) has jazz,
has fez, has got to go. If the word would

be handcuffed and whisked off in cop cars
like those clownish handcuffed killers
on crack on prime time turf, then

technology, efficiency and final-count
mentality must come back strong
with our dark sky behind them.

Apollinaire, Tzara, Breton, Artaud,
Beavis & Butthead, Marilyn Monroe—
the gods will explode with anger

if the Thought-Police persist.
Come back. Oh, come back, baby, come back.
Come back, compose new sites some new sites and comebacks.

PC Mack

DISTANCES

To get to Tokyo from Istanbul,
it's fun to travel when the weather's cool.
To reach Madrid by way of Edinburgh,
it might be best to leave from Glockamorra.

The Shangri-La you dream about comes close
to meeting mute desire—an Ivory Coast,
the Gold Coast of the past, fountains of youth.
All colonies project a light from booths
in darkened rooms of mind; a picture forms
and moves and moves again and spills and warms
spaces between the heartbeat and held breath.

The distance anywhere—from birth to death,
from sit to stand, from heat to holy snow—
invents itself, unravels as you go.

LATE

Thirsty minutes after history has set in
& all the intervals in between
the ticks have dusted time,
you hold court inside your benchless peace.

Sweet contractions of time;
the hour that ripens to your doom.
Ten minutes past the appointed hour
you're still holding your breath.

Fifteen minutes: You hold in your head
several versions at once of what
might have happened, all of them fiction,
none of them buyable, & then

Twenty minutes into the cramp
of time becoming space & voice
you begin to hold this truth as proof,
self-evident: There's no way out.

But quartz has had her way; the ticks,
the tocks their way; the second-hand
takes, the lurching ticks, away, away;
the atom, a splitting of secondary hairs.

You leave your skin. Disaster strikes
this non-event. It's over; birth &
anniversary conspire to set soft
limits on the spread of desire.

And every star will tell you light
is late. If light is late, why wait?
Why turn up early ever every time? Water
parched patience; wet its whistle, waiting.

OCEAN

Green or graying, all the blue breath
you could never expel in song
cannot match the burning light
that smoulders in the fire of my love for you.

Sinewy, stretching, soaked and
rushing still, shy ocean;
slowed-down lover, the color of forever.

The sky of all our longing curls
into an eye and disappears
far across light spread out thin enough to land
where winter neither enters nor departs.

REVIEWING THE SEA

You just don't seem to hug the shore
like you did yesterday; there's more
of a snap to your wash and splash.
Some of us paid cold hard cash
to come all the way out here to rough
old Jersey just to see you do your stuff.

The rating you got in Vacation Guide
might've made a lesser ocean turn and hide;
it was so bad we almost made a change
in plans and toured instead some mountain range—
the Smokies, the Berkshires, the Adirondacks.

But then we walked your sand, saw our tracks
disappear in your rolling wetness, jumped
at your edges until your salt-breath pumped
our lungs free of any clouded, clogging notion
that we could ever freeze or frame your motion.

AIRBORNE

Your beauty, soft Seattle, wasn't subtle;
it turned on light, and seemed at times so cracked,
Rainier could hold her head above your rubble
of cloud and sky alike; erased, snowpacked.

To places where the world once disappeared
we fly. Wild water helps; big clearings don't.
The turns your thighs and belly took are smeared
and jammed with journeys you still say you want
to end. But that's the catch: You like it wet.

You like life darkened, muted; islands, space
and breathing room. From up here all you get
is what I see: You've lost your quiet race
to come in last. Your subtleties are growing.
But night light slows, you know. So how's it going?

SEX AND THE COMMON COLD

The way men start feeling sorry for themselves
at first sign of a cold—my Ph.D thesis
in a coconut shell.

Hell leaves off where Heaven
begins. Those old movies they used to show
in grade school about germs and viruses invading
the body, politic and perm, pay off in knowledge
dollars right here in the College of Costly
21st Century "ahh-chooo!" And the relatively un-
academic "The Story of Jute" never benefitted me
as much as "Sex and the Common Cold." Of course
they never let the narrator of such animated action
say anything much, say anything real we kids could
connect with. They never showed us boogers or snot,

never showed us pool water dripping off of half-
and full-moons in the lockerroom, or the way
language splays and splits like a melon cupped
not once but twice upon a Chaucer. So that when
you come right back down to basics, to the Body
(Part) Electric as salty old Walt might have put it,
then here men go feeling sorry for themselves again.
And for no reason. Not even a magazine ad's worth
of digitized computer-graphed, glamourized mini-blues
hits the arctic spot where cold-germs live; the tinkle
of little squared ice-cubes equals the square root
of sneeze. And who hasn't squeezed their lover,
cold or no cold, deep into the night, trying to suck
from their lips the fever of 42nd St, Tienemin Square?

PC Mack

MORE MOON

We've known each other far too long to lean
against some wall, to brood or sulk. Let's talk
again the way we did when trees were green,
and you were all the distance I could stalk
before your pull, your magnetizing tug
unearthed me; threw me off and laid calm claim
to all the orbits I would ever hug.
I'm calling you again, moaning your name:
Moon, speak, and let your luscious light be known.
Let light, a match-head, scratch our backs in flame.
We've fired each other up, we've thrown our own
and others' voices clean across black skies.
We've bopped and bathed together, bungled deals,
survived. So now let's do what no one tries—
let's roll our chariots out, see how that feels.

STATEMENT ON POETICS

Music—with which poetry remains eternally intimate—seems a dead ringer, as it were, for life itself. And while each also seems invisible, I always catch myself asking: What is life but spirit; spirit-thought made hearable, seeable, smellable, touchable, and delectable?

Who hasn't sung or listened deeply to songs, re-lived recordings, or melted into some performance to the point of identifying almost irretrievably not only with the sound and inner look and feel of music, but with all of its inexplicable beauty; the rapture, the crazy, life-quickening sense of it?

"Man," Jackie McLean told Pacifica Radio's Art Sato in a late 1980s interview, "if we wanna sound like airplanes...we can be an airplane, man." McLean was recalling the reluctance of trumpeter Lee ("The Sidewinder") Morgan to parachute into terrain he hadn't even surveyed before, much less explored. With trombonist-composer Grachan Moncur III, they were rehearsing Moncur's modal, eerie-sounding "Air Raid" for the ground-clearing 1960s Blue Note album, *Evolution.*

"So," McLean is supposed to have said to Morgan, his longtime soul-buddy, "let's be an airplane, you know. 'Cause Grachan is different, man. He likes Frankenstein and Donald Duck and a wide variety of topics, weird topics to write music to."

As Mary Shelley's 1817 horror story and Walt Disney's cartoons have inspired movies, costumes, whole philosophies and music, so music routinely provides poets with *"a wide variety of topics, weird topics."*

Like jazz players and all the other artists and poets, I want to fly, to sail, to leap and jump and jaywalk; I want to walk, skate, surf, skateboard or ski across barriers. If I play Gene Ammons' "Canadian Sunset" and Thelonious Monk's "Carolina Moon" back to back, can you imagine how an escaped slave must have felt once she actually reached Toronto or Montreal? How powerfully odd she must have felt to look back at herself, plotting this break; back there outside Raleigh or Charlotte, where the passing thought of Canada was a dream.

I want to zoom forward and at the same time be watching everything rush by me through the porthole blue of some cloud-blown sky-ship. Or, backlit, seated at the window of a train, Duke Ellington's favorite composing site, I have no trouble seeing and hearing centuries whiz past.

Einstein had it pegged; the mover isn't always necessarily moved by all this movement. Grounded in stillness, rooted in silence, all motion, like sound, feels hopelessly yet deliciously relative. Even so, the beauty of all these scheduled and improvised arrivals and departures neither fades nor reaches any point that even remotely resembles a fully orchestrated stop.

Like the advancing hands of a clock closely watched, the action we know as music or poetry will sometimes appear to stand still. But in truth it is only the quiver and shimmer of being profoundly alive and for-real that slows. The sweet, hot solo jam of believing what you hear just plays and thickens and builds.

After 60 years of listening, I still feel as though I can't get started; as though I have so little to say about jazz and the roles all music continues to play in that curtainless sun-room in the mansion of my life, where thinking and telling take bloom.

STRAIGHT NO CHASER

Well, Monk said it straight:
It's out of town when you wait...
He knew the answer;
The town's a dancer.
You know you can't pack up the moment
And take it with you on the road,
So now is the time.

> *—Sally Swisher*
> (from the blues, "Get It Straight";
> instrumentally known as
> "Straight No Chaser")

STRAIGHT NO CHASER

What wound up seeming strange to you was me.
But why? You bad-mouthed me all over town,
then turned around and asked me if I'd be
your lover one more time. So we got down.

It felt real good. Baby, didn't it? Being real?
Our river overflowed, our tree limbs shook.
The woods, a stormy sky—hey, no big deal!
I wrapped myself around you, then you took

your own sweet time and mine coming unglued.
Pinned down that way, I couldn't tell you off.
You broke our bond, but stuck there in the mood.
To woo or not to woo? My voice went soft.

We slept all slow, got back to work by ten.
I bet you're wondering if I'll call again.

BLUE MONDAY

The blues blow in their purity
more than minds; blues blow
through every sky and haunted heart
afloat. They say: I miss you, baby,
so I really went out and got drunk.

Blues say: Fool that I am, I jam
you in my toaster burning-brown
like bread on fire, blackening
in the Afro red Cadillac flame of love.

Blues say: Baby, you supposed to *be.*
Blues say: You supposed to be so big,
so bad, so slick. Quick! Tell me,
what is the distance from your heart
    to your dick?

109

ERUDITION

And all the worlds and mine
get centered by and by
by clever pundits of the printed world
O hallelujah Dante knew his Popes
and Florentines but Islam no

To even think Muhammad
infernalized seems almost as negligent
as Pope Gregory's error in dispatching
back to Cathay with Marco Polo
not the 100 scholars Kubla Khan requested
to sell his cultured court on Christian grace.
Instead the Pope sent two peevish priests
who didn't withstand the rigors of the trip

TO BATHE OR NOT TO BE

for jim johnson

The water looks just perfect,
the suds just right,
the temperature: moderate to Cool Hand
    Lukewarm.
But steam is not the only stuff that rises here.
Look at all that smoke, the fingers;
a welder's fingers bronze with nicotine.

This is how the man relaxes after work.
Listen to how his slow lawnmower snore cuts
moments off the seconds and snips the minutes
    of his descent.

Would you throw pearls at this divinity?
Would you knowingly give this fellow a light?
Can you even tell if he'll survive
the drowsing waterline now drawn up near
        his tarry lower lip?

The water is perfect;
only the man is pretending to be
asleep. What he awaits is soap to wash
his fuzzy mouth clean out. And then,
all choked up like yesterday, the night before
or every time he dozes in the tub,
he will awake, snorting his gratitude,
buried in the wettened ash of his delight.

THE BUDDHIST WAY OUT WEST REFLECTS ON BOOTS

The loveliness of poems is that they keep;
the loveliness of lives is that they don't.
The rising tide one-ups the tide that falls
—almost.

            You come to me in nothing
but boots and body-mind. Here blue matches
everything you wear or even think
in this improvised December of cold feet;
a wrinkling cold, twice-iced; now tough as lust.
Your soulful earrings' blue goes smoothly with
the blurred blue of our clouded afternight.

Up one-way streets desire has sniffed us down,
and wired us to this alternating force
for keeps. And yet who knows what anguished tide
will swoop tomorrow up and take us out?

So quickly even poetry (our tree-root deep identity)
can't ride time's wave unthrown. The mystery of love
can't hide for long, either. Come melt my night.

Forget today. Let tides and lives be on
their drunken way. Peel off your sea- and sky-
dyed duds; unstrap your blues and stay awhile.
But don't you, don't you, don't you touch them boots!

RIVERS OF LOVERS

after Jan Bailey

The forward flow and rush of Paris by the Seine
and all the Thames, gone by all their names,
rest deep inside the grand Canadian heart Americaine.

There in that yearning season dampened by time and breath
you wait for me just as you've done for centuries;
no Old Man Show Boat River, you, but royal; real.

You unreel just for me inside this phony faked-out world
of phantoms, and take forever to unfold your golden map.
Goodness comes wrapped in you; no foil, no bows.

For all the consequence of steering clear and straight.
I come back knocking time and time again;
arrive continuously at your door and, more,

your windows open wide to unstreaked, sacred views.
Or, rather, all the ways you have of reminding me
of communion fly home to raise the roof, to roost.

You are the night wrapped all around me now;
the sea a drowner battles in the icy midst of night.
You are the midst whose bullseye I must gauge

and strike to break out free of yesterday.
Tomorrow's frightened moon—that too is you
undecked and zigzag in the lightning afternoon.

You are the lightning, the tomorrow and the flashing
    afternoon;
the mind we think is ours, and all we see and smell
and touch and taste and watch. You are the catch.

WHILE WE WATCH

> *after years of living in*
> *Harold Neal's paintings*

Without so much as a *c'est la vie*
an eye becomes a juicy, just-so sigh,
the sigh a why, the why a how,

the how the now of it when we send
each other such musk-filled flowers
of lustful affection. Supple directions

(paint's nippled treasure-load) unfold.
Sierra Madre, you better look out!
Veined with gold and cloud-seeded,

the way a nude indigo or silver jazz
or a Star of David flowers, you might not
come out looking like you look in mirrors.

Errors get corrected as this master
works and maps our blue-ceilinged abandon.
The whole soul domes over with pictures

that quiver and tremble with filigree.
And then the just-you-just-me aspects
of passion come home to roost and root.

BEETHOVEN: "MOONLIGHT" SONATA,
Adagio sostenuto

Who says the lake is often oblivious to moonlight?
And when was light ever lake-shy?
In starry nights and afternoons of 1920, light meant
more than it seems to now in the 1990s
    of unlakely opinions and conditions.

This very Lake Superior might even have been
a cousin or great-grand-cousin to the caw of crow
lake we lap up now and test with toes outspread.

Brrr, the warm chill of these moonless mornings:
Proof that tide takes pride in presence and absence.
Love lives in wet and dried off light alike—ask fishes.

FALLA: NIGHTS IN THE GARDENS OF SPAIN
(Noches en los Jardines de España)

What hot-blooded sound is this?
The castanet languor of Spain forever
pours through insides of me
no color could ever collapse.

A word about color and its headedness:
There is a coolness to red
about which little ever gets said.

Sad, isn't it? I know the Spain
of 1492, when all the Moors and Jews
got sent packing, scrambled abroad
for the sake of *sangre limpia*—
clean-blooded, warmed-over, askance
and all askew, the way we knew when
and where to say Spain.

          How these dances
charm us in sprinkles of step and sweat
and the no-letup silence poured upon us
all salty and spiced; a warming breeze
    straight out of Málaga!

RAVEL: BOLERO

Unraveling Ravel is no longer a secret;
it's all how you plop yourself
in the Spanishness of all this French
kissing in public

Dance !
That's what they say—the flute,
the muter of emotions older than time,
can dance itself.
Clarinet me that one,
Mister Tromborrorooney.

Ay, the clean, brown plains and slopes
of Spain forever Spain forever gallant
forever picaresque.

Saxophone says: I got your pictures;
I got my angles on all of this
and you're all full of steam—

Love is neither now nor
has it ever been tender;
it's castanets; it's the gypsy
of forever who takes you for a ride,
    my friend,
and hits you up for keeps.

OUT OF HAND

Losing this hands-on, candled touch
doesn't really mean what it seems.
Mostly it means that there's so much
still I can glean from dreams.

The sweat I wiped off, doing
all that needed to be done, expired
before I even felt it flowing
from whichever part of me was tired.

MISSISSIPPI MYSTERIES, CONTINUED

Papa wasn't no fool, but neither was that farm.
You could stand nights on the front or back porch
and look clean into Heaven. Papa knew this.
Mama knew it, all the kids, the mules, cows,
chickens, goats, and all the cornstalks knew it.

Oh, God, why do you go around and around inventing
these worlds where birth must come to death,
where silence and slow time saw through all
feelings, all gravied thoughts; the bridges
we must cross but can't build on? If a tropical,
melony breeze came whooshing across the briarpatch
and tickled me sadly, it was because we were in July,
that hellacious month of jubilant weather nights.

OLD TRANE, SAN DIEGO

1/

Under the RR Bridge
a silly even fickle sonance
dances & brings us all around
to rounder, sounder ways of hearing
what the heart flowers
in her private midnight-cum-dawn
hours unobserved. Under Capricorn.
Clouds bring us closer to the dark
sweetmeat of our basic yearning.
Crying, the soul snaps again &
again in dancing clusters of jazz
again, jazz again revolved around
the saxophonic night. Hey, it's
the 20th Century in North America
—almost 21. Do you know
where your promises went? Or what
sky is telling us what?
Hug me quickly and tell me what
I've needed for so long to hear.

Trains' whistles blow in one color only
—blue. And there was no bluer bellow
than the one that comforted me at India
& Date Streets, Little Italy, the strangest
hot January since 1906. Back east the 50-degree
below zero trend was taking off, but
in my room at La Pensione, I was running
the ceiling fan & wondering why I hadn't brought
suntan lotion, That blue-black diesel call
poured into my bed, my coffee, my bath, my bags,
my head & all the books I lay there reading;
the cloud-blue sky protecting Little Italy
by day, the Lamplight District nights.
Downtown, the home of homelessness,
in the 99 cents store, a curious young woman,
all brown & tan, Mexico-born, eyed me up & down
& laughed when I talked to her of earthquake skies.
She might've been remembering Mexico City
the year the whole mountainside trembled
and it all caved in.

But it was my Spanish;
the very word *terremoto,* a little like
Quasimodo—monsters, both—that made her laugh;
that made me world-weary giggly a halfday late.
At 4:31 a.m. my single hotel bed already had
turned into a waterbed, so strong was the song
L.A. was blowing. "Here we go again," I told
San Diego. "Haven't we ridden this freight car
before? Why didn't your horn sound a warning?"

DROWNING IN THE SEA OF LOVE
(Fragment)

Fathom after fathom
the fullness of being no place else
emptiesme to love

There's no other way to explain
this zoom this taking
leave which is really giving
leave without notice
or the other way around

It's hard to even breathe under
all this sea & seeing
much less swim or float

And so floating deeper
deeper the surface blurs
& tunnels gold and blue
with glittering entrances and
ways to new worlds bubble up

Fathom after fathom
the bones lighten the blood
lets air & warmth curl
around night-questions
answerable at daylight level
until soon there is no more
leaving no more coming back
green with newness only
the hum of peaceful heat
inside one ear the madness
of water making its choices
all at once afterwards
in the rush defying aftermath
fathom after fathom

A HYMN TO HER

(Divine Mother)

Like some swollen, swaying samba
under pressure to behave,
you are wild and without number;
neither principle nor wave.

Can your dance subdue its dancers
when we dancers are the song?
Can your slow, half-whispered answers
float us back where we belong?

Everything we long or ache for is
within soothing reach, it seems.
You surround us with your wakefulness;
you astound us in your dreams.

WRITTEN IN BRACING, GRAY L.A. RAINLIGHT

It seems to be the time of bad gigs,
low pay, no-pay and no-shows.
Even the weary palms that line thin air-
port arcades aren't buying this light.
Busted, sleepy, hungry and blank,
the I who was, am ready for take-off.

Heaven after all is right next door;
its chilling warmth alive in time
to the swish and meter of longed-for rain
in our fourth long year of drought.

True, everybody talking about heaven
ain't going there. But if I ever
get my hands on good money again,
the price of light is going to rise
and shine. And, hear me, I ain't paying.

DHAKA, BANGLADESH

In Muslim countries, monumental choices
must be made and stuck to palmishly,
under overheated skies the way
old Moorish fountains flowed and flowered
in Granada. That is, this is poetry,
my friend, on a silvery, windblown morning
not all that far from Mecca.

My name is Dhaka. Here all the leg-and-motor-
powered rickshaws sport eye-winning artwork
painted on directly in colors that yellow
your blue-green readiness to roll
right over Jordan. And when it rains,
you'll sometimes glimpse the sleek, brown,
blackening bodies of our drivers glide by
right on time, thronged with sweat-swept solemnity.

Here human mules and mullahs alike meet up,
brush up, jam into one another; here where
your mother, your sister, your brother and
all your thirsty cousins gathered five times daily
to shovel in at ear-splitting levels the voice
of the imam, loudspeakered and commanding.
In gravelly blares that pebble the air
with prayer, he declares: Amin, Amin, Amin.

FAIRBANKS, ALASKA

for Peggy Shumaker

Blessed are the angels and their crystalline sound
wound around my head in bed the night I lay me down
finally in Fairbanks after 24 mad hours in Anchorage.
And what is this music and these heightened states
I love so? Sacred ground and sacred air; sacred
mountains all snuggled and mufffled in sacred snow.
Chanting, breathing, polar-needled kundalini yoga—
it all plays off magnetically in arctic blasts of silence.

FIFTY-FIFTY

for Donald S. Ellis

By fifty, you know who you are and, more,
you almost know what you don't know. Perhaps.
You know your body-house—its roof, its floor;
know what it lacks, its leaks, its loose backsteps.
And sometimes, up alone, safe in the dark,
a Friday dinner savored, jazz, some beers—
the livingroom your camp, sweet home your park—
you drowse and dream. Remembering the dares
a younger you fulfilled without a flinch,
you picture where your children will grow old.
On 21st Century turf, each one will inch
by inch construct some crazy, brave household.
You wonder what they'll have or know of you,
who took six decades learning what do to.

DRUNK ON RIMBAUD'S BOAT

for Barry Gifford

While all his ships sailed in, Arthur sank.
For this he had himself to thank.
Does light salute the measured dark's
gold cargo hauled on silver arks?
Love, then, became industrialized,
and poetry, no longer prized,
withdrew from his untidy shore.
Slave-running, guns, hashish, and more
kept him in Africa; swept up.
With all his hunches played, he stopped.

Paris 1992

BIG SKIES, BIG LIGHT

an epithalamion for
Alan and Kris Cheuse

The hills, the climb, the tricky roads, a ranch
that overlooks the sea; big skies, big light—
the perfect setting for an avalanche;
the slip and slide of love from outward height
to soul-defying depths. The mind alone
has trouble keeping track of what it means
to write this down, or dance it, blood and bone,
even while the heart pumps music to such scenes.
Mere thought and flesh and feeling cannot hold;
like clouds, they float, thin out and trail away.
Spirit, the jewel of love, its oldest gold,
forever virginal, hides night and day.
Its secret, though, is this: It loves to dance
and marry with itself—divine romance.

OCTOBER WITH O.O.

There seemed to have been another version
of October I was after, maybe the one Goldie Hawn
abandoned when she joined the wrong army.
Private Benjamin, forgive me, but crazy doesn't quite
explain the night I'm tucked in here to hear.

Instead of paying attention to my condition,
blanketed down as I am with autumn love,
my smoothed-out thoughts are cruising and
schmoozing. Fantasies and bigtime jealousies
hang out with me on this night of tropical loss.

"I been thinking bout going back," O.O. says,
"and getting me one of them big Michigan women."
"O.O., what on earth are you talking about?"
"Talking bout love," he says. "Talking bout earth.
Talking bout a for-real, big-bone, substantial-
looking woman got farmgirl hips and great big legs;
move just like she walking on soft-boiled eggs."

This isn't mine; this was O.O.'s October.
Women he's cruising and schmoozing right now
got their own ideas about this. They'd kiss
October adiós and au revoir as soon as frame it;
that is, if it didn't represent what they meant.

Ann Arbor 1992

OUR LITTLE LIFE IS ROUNDED WITH A SLEEP

William Shakespeare,
The Tempest, *Act 4, Scene 1*

Impossible dreamers entertain impossible dreams.
They wink and blink at you in colors you know
but hardly ever see change. Mimicries of the gone
world seem to line the seams of every dreamer's
dream and soul-lit pillow. Shakespeare knew.
"To sleep perchance to dream" might very well
have been his way of having Hamlet say
what Zulu ancients knew: When you are alive
it is the same as when you are dead, and dead
you are the same as when you are alive.
Entertain that, but don't forget Othello
dreamed the impossible when he eloped with Desdemona
to simply live. No happily ever after; no stop, no go.

NURSERY LINES FOR A PLANTER

Other times it's the very way
the moon slips you
into memories of flying at will
anyplace you wanna go. Veracruz
will do, or maybe an overnight
at the Hotel Jupiter, an ocean
slosh away from many nowheres.
Can there be such a place
without the whole notion sounding
corny? Moon & memory are like that.
So are thoughts, & all the aughts
you oughtta clear before you go
moooon, like a milkcow mooing
at noon in June atop a sad dune.
O the pleasures of everyday English!
It's enough to make a poor lovesick dish
take up & run away with a spoon.

SEEING RED

You always seem to get it all wrong about me.
Just like in the days back when you thought
you'd up and die if you chomped me down,
so you ate my leaves instead and wound up dead.
Now you think it's OK to keep me from dying,
so you actually poison me through irradiation.
Where's your imagination? Where's the spirit
of the Aztecs, who grew me to death, named me tamatl,
and loved me for the very fruity berry that I am?
From Plato to NATO, the vegetable consciousness
of Western Civilization mineralizes its own
pockets; oil-cloth pockets so you can steal soup.
That growers in this nation would stoop
to chemotherapy to give me greater so-called shelf-
life may hold the answer to cancer, but it doesn't
do a thing for me. I like to salt and spice
your mouth up, then seed it all red with zesty juice
and yellow-green after-thoughts like the bright
ting-a-ling of love. You hear what I'm saying?
You hear what I'm telling you? Rather than right
those ancient wrong notions, you've motioned them on.
Like edible street gangsters now, rain or shine,
we don't die; we multiply. Tell Henry Heinz
we tumorless tomatoes constantly see the best minds
of our generations goosed, juiced, and pissed.

TIPPING IS NOT A CITY IN CHINA

And neither is a nose-ring, my dear,
or is it? Surely the sun that grows
on trees and all the shadows that tip
afternoon towards twilight understand.

But what this tipping means in Nanking
or Beijing is Greek to both of us.
Australia makes it clear: Please don't tip;
we pay our workers well. Even Marco Polo
knew his catches well when it came to Cathay.
Ask Genny Lim, who grew up in Chinatown
San Francisco imagining New York. "All that food
you Italians boast about came from my ancestors,"
she makes clear. Spaghetti, my dear, can't be
the only dish unraveling here.

                            One last tip:
Water isn't the worst item not on the menu
to offer a thirsty traveler; nor a smile.
I didn't mean to break into your phone chat
with Rahshid when I signalled for the tab,
but you can tell him I apologize.
Tell him this for me too: While I do admire
the way you strut your lovely stuff,
I can't recall service worse than yours
since that time in Taiwan I asked them for water
and, so help me Howlin' Wolf, they brought me
    gasoline.

ADAGIO

And where in this spring of sleepy dread
does love live now? In the breathing
mausoleum of that space you call heart?
In the slow-voiced poet part of you, perhaps?
Or, better, in the pirouette of time itself,
which turns or twists on love, you know.

Or do you know anything at all anymore,
you who watch and listen so carefully and

sip your buttermilk in vivid ambidexterity
before the windows of this throbbing afternoon,
whose light can only be the false friend of puppies?

Come, quench the A-bomb tension of my urge
to touch and soften you. Please answer me.
Please ferret from the gristle of your sneer
some bone-chip I could masticate; something
sharp yet chewy enough to mean: "I forgive."

THE GOSPEL TREES, DETROIT

Trees
of hunger
trees of root & sky their tentacles
so strong & strange & straight
they uplift light up leaf
beneath the smoke cloud cover
of gospel bass

Hovering

In thin air

so thick
these
trees
don't
need
to
see
to
breathe
or
stand

ULTRAVIOLET

for joan Lederman

Light sizzling in clay
collects. The river moves
the way sun shows—
points in that direction.
Solar water muddies the glaze
of heat and its ceramics
long before someone's hands.
"Tell her what the shape I'm in,"
sang Sonny Terry, sharing
song with Brownie McGhee.
"I have had my fun," the song goes,
"if I don't get well no more."
And that, the way of all songs,
can't help but hang beyond the sun
& all the leaves it takes with it;
bug-buried clay alive with ultra-
violet light. Is there a night?

THE ONE SNAPSHOT I COULDN'T TAKE IN FRANCE

Shot through with silver gray light,
waylaid by big-bellied bridges,
this France is not for sale. Not this
Paris, where they serve nothing but French
classics at the Polidor in Rue Monsieur
Le Prince, Richard Wright's favorite.
Hell, he lived right up the street.
We talking about the Paris where you get on
the bus and the draft you feel ain't coming
from no open windows. And while you sit,
soaking up aisle light and the street-lit faces
of passengers, you know you're neither welcome

nor wanted. Excusez-moi! Oui, you're in the way.
Your heart is busy feeling up the back pages
of places faraway, your mental roadblocks;
atlases Ayn Rand could've never shrugged off.

POSTCARDS FROM MONTANA

KALISPELL

The rambling, wide-skyed beauty of this town
looks up for grabs. When people just don'tcare,
how quickly fast-food ugliness can ruin
the rain, unearth the soil and wreck the air.

YELLOW BAY

1/

Outside, where the lake begins
and all Montana ends, I laugh
under the trees with you.
Our tiny-weathered model of life
leaves us with no silver, no chalice
of wet light shining in the sound
of being here. The lake begins
to swallow itself and blue sun flees.
Where but in the slowed-down sex
of Yellow Bay bees would sweetness
taste itself running up a mountainside
and down again to where the lake begins?

2/

Golden openings light the way
afternoon, afternight and day;
this is more than I'd expected,
this Montana feels protected.

3/

Such open-ended mountain paths are where
Babaji and ancient yogis share
their love of God, inseparable from themselves;
a love too vast to fit or sit still on book
    shelves.

LOS ANGELES, LOS ANGELES:
One Long-Shot, One Cutaway

1/

Inside your belly, a new beast ripens.
While all your twilit litters guard the door,
the ghost of Ho Chi Minh pours out a toast:

Here's to old Saigon, Taiwan, Hong Kong, Beijing;
Iran before the Shah; to Port-au-Prince,
and Port of Spain, Tijuana, Kingston Town;
to Tokyo, Bombay, Tel-Aviv, Nairobi and Accra.

Not Ghana but the oldest Gold Coast drums
her thoughts out loud in not so cooling colors,
The darkest nights of Seoul turn into tunnels,
where rays of hope, spaghetti thin, break skin
and ream the veins of dreams so long deferred

that laser-lined Thought Police 100 years from now
still can't decrypt the meaning of their blood;
    their blues.

2/

A Stoly on the rocks, some rock cocaine,
a spoon of smack can crack the sound of barriers
and barrios alike. But light is hard.

MEMORY MEANDERS, AND SOMETIMES MEOWS

The bark of habit's for the dogs;
obsequious toadies, Uncle Toms.
But memory, more tit than tat,
feels feline; fickle as a feather.

The cat inside us purrs; curled
up, up—poised to pounce,
or stretch or lick herself;
alight at the drop of a litter.

Memory, the mammary gland of kit,
kaboodle, both, behaves that way.
All eyes and fur, she'll take you
for a ride. Or slink. Or hide.

Author's note

*As a concluding gesture, I have selected two poems from
the gifted language poet F.C. Mack's curious underground
sensation,* The Purina Elegies. *And, to restructure credit where
credit is due, I must also acknowledge the poet O.O. Gabugah,
that African American maverick, who first alerted me to Ms.
Mack's poetry. Moreover, O.O. seems to have had the pleasure
of taking a summer workshop with the poet while she was
Writer-in-Residence at the Cool School's Overseas Program
in Northern Studies at Reykjavik, Iceland.*

A.Y.

LANGUAGE LIKE MY HALF-BLIND CAT MELISSA

This wave of caring
yellow orange or red
greens up the spectrum
mandolin: Vivaldi,
look out! No doctorate
for just buying the books
and hanging out you know.
Language like my half-blind cat
Melissa limps electric
through the snow. She melts
the garnered fruits we note,
recording angels that we are,
and shivers. Soft usage
understands the pulp of poetry
pitted against the windowed ear.
No form but this: the thrills
of cat-and dog-walking alone,
or to fish perhaps and outbait
the master, Beta of them all.
In red already. Better yet
to yellow-bait or play

your plectrum at the lectern,
while oranges fly straight at you.
Or make good grief turn green
with more than envy. For Melissa
those Roman or Neapolitan goodbyes
just mean it's time to dine.
Unless you wave. Take care.

BUFFALO NICOLE

Yuck, Nicole, you striped bimbo of cats.
With all this slushed up snow stacked up
and up and up all damaged now with soot
and gasoline, you choose to meow the blues
at sunrise by your empty dish. Fuck hunger!
When twilight falls this cold in Buffalo
I'll hold my breath before I run out
of rhymes or schemes to make you scream
Uncle! Sometimes when the kitty litter
lights up in the dark, I realize
that even if I hit the Big Lotto
or pulled the wheel right on the Big Spin
there's just no way I'd ever give you up.
Nicole, you fabulous feline of whispering
whiskers, come curl up by me in this Baby
It's Cold Outside milieu. Blaze me
out of this blizzard of Is You Is
or Is You Ain't. You know you'll always be
my cat—and, yo, you can snowbank on that.

from The Furina Elegies

AL YOUNG

The author of several previous books of poetry, Al Young is also a novelist and essayist. He is moreover the recipient of NEA, Guggenheim and Fulbright Fellowships as well as the PEN/Library of Congress Award for Short Fiction and the PEN/USA Award for Non-Fiction. A popular reader and performer of his own work (sometimes to music), Young travels and lectures worldwide on literature, music, creativity, the arts, and African American culture and politics.

Among other teaching posts he has held, Al Young has taught writing and literature at Stanford, the University of California at Berkeley, Davis and Santa Cruz, Rice University, the University of Washington, Austin Peay State University, the University of Arkansas, and the University of Michigan.

Young wrote and narrated the legendary video documentary, *Color: A Sampling of African American Writers.* He annotated and contributed tracks to Rhino's *Our Souls have Grown Deep Like the Rivers (Black Writers Read Their Work)* as well as *In Their Own Voices: A Century of Recorded Poetry.* He is a regular contributor of CD liner notes for the Verve Jazz Masters series.

VIVIAN TORRENCE

Since 1992, Chicago-born artist Vivian Torrence has lived in Munich. Her acclaimed collages, watercolors, drawings and prints have been widely exhibited in museums and galleries throughout the United States and, more recently, in Europe. Included in private collections (the Hallmark Corporation, Kansas City, and the Continental Corporation of New York), her work is also featured in such public collections as the Art Institute of Chicago, the Des Moines Art Center, and the Hirshhorn Museum in Washington, DC.

Torrence, whose teaching career began at Iowa State University, has been a visiting artist and lecturer at the University of California, Berkeley, and the University of Florida as well as a visiting scholar at Cornell. With Nobel chemist and poet Roald Hoffman, she collaborated on *Chemistry Imagined: Reflections on Science.* In his introduction, the late Carl Sagan wrote: "Vivian Torrence responds to the beauty, mystery and utility of chemistry in a striking set of collages."

Of her recent collage, "Moments Are Feathers," this book's cover, Torrence says: "Al Young's poetry has a quality of mysticism that continues to inspire my work."